Lewis.Tsurumaki.Lewis

Lewis.Tsurumaki.Lewis

Opportunistic Architecture

Paul Lewis, Marc Tsurumaki, David J. Lewis

Graham Foundation for Advanced Studies in the Fine Arts
Chicago

Princeton Architectural Press
New York

Graham Foundation / Princeton Architectural Press series

New Voices in Architecture

presents first monographs on emerging designers from around the world

Published by
Princeton Architectural Press
37 East Seventh Street
New York, New York 10003

For a free catalog of books, call 1.800.722.6657.
Visit our website at www.papress.com.

Photo credits:
Michael Moran: 13, 25, 27, 28 left, 32 right, 33–34, 35 top right, 46–49, 51 top right, 52–57,
    58 bottom left, 63, 76, 78 right, 79, 80 right, 81, 83–87, 131, 133 top, 134, 135 bottom, 158–59,
    160–66, 167 top right
Rudolph Janu: 29–31, 34 top right
Elliott Kaufman: 112 bottom, 114 bottom, 115 bottom
Hye-Young Chung: 137
Maya Galbis: 58 top left, 132, 167 bottom
dbox: 152 top left, 154 bottom, 157 bottom right

LTL would like to thank Hilary Zaic, Maya Galbis, Elizabeth Hodges, Alex Terzich, Beatie Blakemore,
Jason Dannenbring, Tamicka Marcy, and Kathryn van Voorhees for their work on this book.

Editor: Dorothy Ball
Design: LTL with Jan Haux

Special thanks to: Nettie Aljian, Sara Bader, Nicola Bednarek, Janet Behning, Becca Casbon, Penny (Yuen
Pik) Chu, Russell Fernandez, Pete Fitzpatrick, Wendy Fuller, Clare Jacobson, John King, Nancy Eklund Later,
Linda Lee, Laurie Manfra, Katharine Myers, Lauren Nelson Packard, Jennifer Thompson, Arnoud Verhaeghe,
Paul Wagner, Joseph Weston, and Deb Wood of Princeton Architectural Press —Kevin C. Lippert, publisher

Library of Congress Cataloging-in-Publication Data
Lewis, Paul, 1966–
  Lewis.Tsurumaki.Lewis : opportunistic architecture / Paul Lewis, Marc Tsurumaki, David J. Lewis. —
1st ed.
    p. cm. — (New voices in architecture)
  ISBN-13: 978-1-56898-710-1 (alk. paper)
  ISBN-10: 1-56898-710-2 (alk. paper)
  1. Lewis.Tsurumaki.Lewis—Themes, motives. 2. Architecture, Modern—21st century. I. Tsurumaki,
Marc, 1965– II. Lewis, David J., 1966– III. Title.
  NA737.L454L47 2007
  720.92'2—dc22
                                                          2007002186

Contents

Introduction

By definition, the word *opportunistic* has negative connotations, referring to the seizing of any circumstances regardless of principles or ethics. In our selective use of this term, we invoke the active agency this word implies as it might pertain to architecture, while seeking to invert the dubious moral implications in service of an open, generative, and creative approach to work. We seek opportunistic overlaps between form, space, program, material, and budget, teasing design invention out of the rich potential latent within the restrictions and limits that frame architecture.

Lewis.Tsurumaki.Lewis (LTL) is an architectural practice driven by a curiosity about the world and optimistic about the architect's role in shaping the built environment. We aim to create a practice that is simultaneously critical and engaged, working between these often polarized positions in the discourse of architecture. We are interested in an approach to architecture that exists beyond either critical resistance or complicity. This requires agility and cunning on the part of the architect—a willingness to playfully engage the rules, bending and pushing them through the rigorous application of logic to create the extraordinary. It is simultaneously pragmatic and speculative, carefully examining and acknowledging existing structures while working through invention and new possibilities. This approach situates the architect not as utopian visionary or dutiful professional but as equal parts alchemist and realist, operating not through grand gestures but with wit and an intelligence informed by thorough research, using the potential of architecture to transform and invent. To do so we have sought to establish a flexible and nimble method of work that addresses each project both critically and optimistically: looking to maximize the opportunities inherent in the conditions of a given project rather than superimpose a priori a set of expectations that would immediately confine and restrict its potential.

Working opportunistically, we undertake an intentionally wide range of projects, from small installations to speculative propositions and larger institutional buildings, independent of size, program, or cost, with a proportionally equal investment of research into the expectations and conditions that frame and establish the architectural question at hand. For instance, smaller installations or exhibitions—10 Shades of Green, Parking Sections, and Refiled—address the challenges of siting architecture within the constraints of changing museums or display venues. Larger institutional or public buildings, including Arthouse, Bornhuetter Hall, and Building 82%, require an engagement with the particulars of program, budget, site, client needs, and code. Restaurant projects—Dash Dogs, Fluff, Ini Ani, Lozoo, Tides, and Xing—come to terms with the challenges of working within existing spaces, where the dictates of seating and service reduce the area of experimental design to the thickened surfaces of the walls and ceilings. The speculative projects—New Suburbanism, Park Tower, and Tourbus Hotel—unburdened by budgets or client expectations, explore the opportunities and pleasures of representation while examining emergent cultural conditions as a catalyst for new typologies and forms.

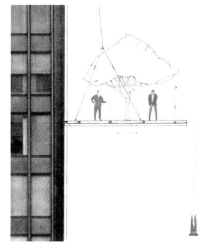

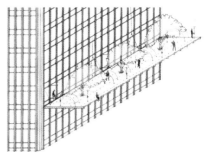

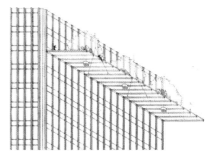

Mies-on-a-Beam

What if the cleaning system for the windows of the Seagram building was considered a landscape supplement, returning function to the two anomalous, nonfunctional aspects of the building: the I-beams and the tree plaza? How can one do more with less-is-more?

We seek to bring all projects to a point of realization where their impact within the world can be made legible, either through material fabrication and construction or through careful development in drawings, models, and hybrid forms of architectural representation. In addition to operating in the more traditional role of realizing buildings with outside contractors or builders, we have often built portions of projects ourselves, directly engaging in the crafting of walls, surfaces, and objects—a situation necessitated in some cases by constrained schedules and limited budgets. More importantly, our interest in testing the potential for a project compels us to move beyond the typical boundaries of the profession to explore spatial and material possibilities at full scale, in effect drawing with steel, wood, and felt rather than ink and pencil. We desire to always expand the territory of architectural exploration, experimentation, and invention, and we see the translation between drawing and building as an arena redolent with potential.

Testing 1…2…3…
This installation at Storefront for Art and Architecture explores hybrids between diverse representational techniques: physical models, drawings, and interactive electronics.

In addition to working on projects initiated by clients or through competitions, we have also explored projects that are self-generated. These speculative projects—including New Suburbanism, Tourbus Hotel, and Park Tower—continue work we began early in the formation of the office and published in 1998 in Pamphlet Architecture No. 21, *Situation Normal…* Selected samples of these earlier speculative installations and projects illustrate this introduction. We use these projects to look creatively at architectural programs and types, asking a series of "what if…" questions that tease out architectural play from the desires embedded in programs and types. Recognizing that these projects would be built only through drawings and models, the very logic of architectural representations is the site of their realization (see Tactic: Over Drawing, p. 176). We carefully deploy and develop hybrid systems of representation, exploring new wrinkles in the canon of architecture's visual language. Fundamental to the legibility of these projects then is the capacity of the drawings—made through a combination of digital and hand-drafted techniques—to integrate a demonstration of the project as an architectural object with its underlying conceptual logic.

Applied Curiosity

The work presented in this monograph is arranged alphabetically, not chronologically. This organization introduces a necessary arbitrariness to the reading of the projects, which are not grouped by building type or scale, in order to intentionally set off the logic of invention particular to each project. Causal or temporal threads cannot be read from one project to the next. Each project must be taken on its own terms and seen for the opportunities that have been seized, developed, and tested. Yet unifying the individual projects is our insistence that curiosity, a central component of our architectural practice, plays a consistent and operative role in organizing and challenging research. In this sense, we see curiosity in the manner succinctly expressed by Michel Foucault:

Curiosity is a new vice that has been stigmatized in turn by Christianity, by philosophy, and even by a certain conception of science. Curiosity, futility. The word, however, pleases me. To me it suggests something altogether different: it evokes "concern"; it evokes the care one takes for what exists and could exist; a readiness to find strange and singular what surrounds us; a certain relentlessness to break up our familiarities and to regard otherwise the same things; a fervor to grasp what is happening and what passes; a casualness in regard to the traditional hierarchies of the important and essential.[1]

1 Michel Foucault, "The Masked Philosopher," in *Foucault Live: (Interviews, 1961–1984)*, trans. John Johnson (New York: Semiotext(e) Double Agents Series, 1996), 198–99.

For our practice, curiosity establishes a charged relationship between the specifics of the project at hand and broader cultural, economic, and political discourses, a relationship that is critical and skeptical, yet optimistic and engaged. As such, we maintain that the practice of architecture can be a vital and illuminating enterprise. This is precisely because architecture, of all the discursive fields, is intimately tied into broader economic and political systems. Architecture and the patterns that it engenders form to an extraordinary degree the norms, habits, and frameworks that once established tend to go unnoticed, are typically experienced in a state of distraction, and are thus assumed to be timeless and inevitable rather than fabricated and constructed.

Throughout our work, driven by curiosity, we continually ask the following questions: What if the constraints and limitations of architecture became the catalyst for design invention? What if the conditions that are typically thought to restrict practice are conceptually transformed to become the generator for architectural exploration? These questions encourage an imaginative engagement with the boundaries that define contemporary architecture—limits that are defined through the complex network of cultural values, political imperatives, technological systems, consumer desires, and economic frameworks that invariably circumscribe architectural projects (see Tactic: Catalyzing Constraints, p. 168).

Such a method requires a reconsideration of concepts, inherited from eighteenth-century critiques of the Enlightenment, that maintain that design excellence can only come from a freedom from everyday constraints and obligations. In contrast, we have learned that the most productive architectural theses are framed by their limitations: where the conditions bounding the project are transformed into the very arguments for development; where cost limitations become the opportunity to rethink program diagrams; where aesthetic preconceptions enable a close examination of the historical and cultural meanings embedded in stylistic habits; where material possibilities exist in the redeployment of common materials or objects not typically found within Sweets Catalogues. To do this, we seek the wiggle room within any given project, discovering new opportunities from within rather than imposing a priori expectations from the outside. The driving thesis thus emerges from the dialectic between research and design, where design is coupled with research, directing and reacting in turn to greater specificity and new provocations brought forward through the exchange.

By research, we mean a speculative inquiry, one that is fundamentally open-ended, non-linear, and inquisitive. This expansive form of research combines traditional forms of academic inquiry, utilizing digital and analog methods, brought together with direct access to specialists and knowledgeable professionals from various fields. It requires first-hand engagement and documentation of the conditions of a site and full-scale testing of possible materials and spaces. For this reason, we begin each project through a careful inventory of all known factors, conditions, and expectations before any design proposals are initiated, taking stock of the full range of conditions that mark the rules and boundaries through which the design will be fielded. This research provides a dialectic testing ground, one adaptable and mutable to the contingencies of design and the trajectories that may be taken but are not yet foreseen.

More often than not we discover that our initial expectations are not nearly as provocative as what exists beyond the veil of assumptions. The design of Bornhuetter Hall was generated through an open inquiry into the future of residential housing for a college in a small town in Ohio. We spoke extensively with students, faculty, trustees, and service staff about their concerns and desires, conducted surveys on the existing state of the residential facilities, and studied current trends in residential housing. The information we gathered challenged our initial expectations about what forms best foster increased public student interaction. Further research directed us to the best site for the building from possible locations throughout the campus, which, when brought into conversation with the information on optimal hall size and arrangement, determined to a great extent the overall form and configuration of the building.

Another case in point is Tourbus Hotel. The project was developed through sending a staff member on an all-expenses-paid bus tour through Europe. She collected evidence by videotape of the entire tour through the window of the bus and made a detailed log of actual time spent and locations visited on a typical European bus tour. Not only did this demonstrate that the entire industry of European bus tours re-maps the continent according to the distance a union bus driver is allowed to drive in a day—thus creating major destinations out of accidents of geography, turning the small town of Saint Gore, equidistant from Amsterdam and Lucerne, into a significant stop—but also that, surprisingly, the least amount of time on these tours is actually spent in the destination cities for which the tours are ostensibly created. Moreover, the incompatibility between the size of the tour bus and dense historic cities forces the tours to select hotels outside the city destination. Our approach is not to lament or cynically reveal these idiosyncratic conditions, but rather to see these SNAFUs as rich sites for architectural propositions. Tourbus Hotel, like our other projects, is thus

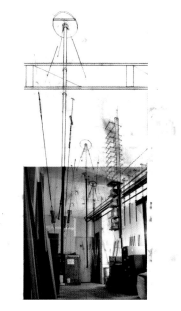

Slip Space

Acknowledging the limits of its gallery context, this installation directly engages only the floor as the site of exchange, support, and structure for three stools, a bookshelf, and a table. Each is placed through the floor, oscillating on springs between the basement below and the gallery above.

dependent on the information produced through active and open inquiry into the multiple facets that frame the subject at hand. This type of work continues throughout the development of any given project, where the direction of inquiry responds to the opportunities opened through the design process, and in turn sites for architectural invention are fostered through research (see Tactic: Invention Sprawl, p. 170).

Even in the approach to exhibition design, where we have been asked to represent our work in exhibition spaces within academic institutions, the end project comes directly out of research we have collected through experience working with the uneven quality of lighting often associated with academic galleries. Instead of ignoring or complaining about this condition, the design for Light Structures builds the entire exhibition around and off a standard 8' fluorescent bulb, making it the central structural spine for the display system, paradoxically supporting the exhibition directly off the light. The bulb provides consistent backlighting for the images, independent from the particular illuminating system of the various galleries into which the show travels.

The possibilities for distinct avenues of research expand with larger and more complex projects. As the role played by architects becomes increasingly entangled on a global scale with systems of production, distribution, and information exchange, all necessary now in bringing a project into realization, there is not only a logistical imperative for research but, we argue, immense creative opportunities in foregrounding research as design, and design as research.

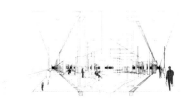

Free Lobby / Block 1290

This project looks closely at the assumptions ascribed to the division between public sidewalk and private lobby, proposing a reconsideration of the urban landscape at street level. Partitions between separate lobbies are removed, producing an open public space that spans the whole block.

Restricted Play

In order to engage these complex limits and constraints through research and design, we recast architectural practice as a form of restricted play.[2] Play is not a frivolous act of secondary importance, but a way of creatively working that calls for rigor while insisting upon perpetual critique and inquiry.[3] Play is the active manifestation of curiosity, operating from a position embedded within the world. To play or to put something in play requires action and commitment, in seeking a goal through transformation and change. In this sense, we see the restricted play of architectural practice as neither a diversion nor removed from life, but rather the constant inquiry into the possibilities and potentials of architecture to have an effect and create anew.

It is impossible, however, to play without rules or, more specifically, without knowing the rules. This is as true for any game played by children as it is for the complex international negotiations at play in the world. Rules provide a shared terrain within which players can engage the issues at hand. In architecture, the rules are numerous, daunting, and often overwhelming. They are political (codes, licenses, regulations, laws), economic (costs, finances, real estate), technical (labor, skill, craft, technique), cultural (precedents, conventions of use, desires), formal (typologies, proportional systems, geometries), and material (gravity, raw resources, ecology), to name only a few. Indeed, architecture as a discipline is defined by rules, standards, and expected forms

2 For additional discussion on the pedagogical value of play as a concept, see David J. Lewis, "Position 1: Newness, Play and Invention." *Scapes* 1 (2002): 20–21.

3 "Here we have at once a very important point: even in its simplest forms on the animal level, play is more than a mere physiological phenomenon or psychological reflex. It goes beyond the confines of purely physical or purely biological activity. It is a significant function— that is to say, there is some sense to it. In play there is something 'at play' which transcends the immediate needs of life and imparts meaning to the action. All play means something." Johan Huizinga, *Homo Ludens* (New York: Beacon Press, 1971), 1.

of work, reinforced by the numerous laws on professional conduct, material properties, construction standards, and code compliance. But whereas professions including law, accounting, and architecture are asked to work within the given rules—to ensure, in fact, that rules are followed and loopholes closed—the task of the architect is also to question norms, rules, and conventions, playing the game to near the breaking point.

In this sense, the restricted play of architecture requires paradoxically holding in balance a careful study of the existing rules of the discipline while advocating for the selective dismantling of those same norms. The ability to hold in creative tension these two opposed conditions is of vital importance. Rote repetition according to given rules reduces architecture to formulaic procedure and policy, while, conversely, ignoring the professional obligations of architecture in pursuit of the perpetually new equates architectural invention with willful personal expression, a situation in which the very ideas of public and environmental responsibility, culture, history, and discipline are essentially irrelevant. By recasting architectural practice as a form of serious play, we seek an expansive architecture born of curiosity and in perpetual inquiry, one that amplifies the pleasure of an experience while enacting a transformation of everyday life. In short, we are interested in the messy tension that exists in the middle of the playing field, being, as it were, caught up in the game.

Multivalent Performance

Working from the methodology proposed above, we strive to produce work that navigates the multiple and often contradictory demands of each project, negotiating the overlapping agendas of program, spatial form, and inhabitation while generating sensory environments that engage the user at diverse levels. Such an architecture operates simultaneously at a rich haptic and optical level while sponsoring a dense range of performances, environmental functions, and social conditons, often within a single form, space, or surface. In this way the functional possibilities of any given component are maximized and synthesized, giving rise to effects that supersede any singular logic or function. For instance, the 3/4-inch-thick walls of Fluff Bakery synthesize the requirements for sound absorption, padded seating, mechanical space, lighting, storage, display, and spatial enclosure to produce a visually seductive surface composed of commonplace, inexpensive materials (see Tactic: Alchemical Assemblies, p. 174). We recognize that any project is a contested and constantly shifting ground where different users will operate in incompatible and overlapping ways, with competing purposes and goals. Therefore, we seek a multifaceted understanding of architectural programs that are not tethered to an isolated moment in time, but are able to adjust and anticipate future uses and needs. We refer to such architecture as exhibiting multivalent performance.

This is a challenge to singular readings, fixed functional equations, and totalizing aesthetic ideologies, as well as the recent turn toward using complex algorithms to

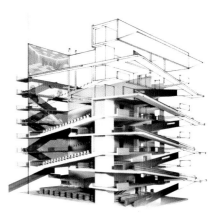

Video Filmplex
What if the distinct architectural programs of movie theater and video store were playfully brought together to form a new hybrid type, seeking opportunistic spatial overlaps between economically dependent media formats?

generate forms, driven by primarily ocular conceits. Instead, we advocate multivalence and an overlapping of uses, experiences, and functions. In many instances, architects are compelled to make one-sided decisions between competing expectations and demands, to choose, for instance, between the market-driven need for new forms at the expense of material longevity, or between historic preservation and contemporary urban uses. For an architecture of multivalent performance, we create projects that play on the pleasures of paradoxes, offering alternatives that don't make simple sacrifices in favor of easy solutions. For instance, in negotiating between institutional expectations for architectural signification and individual use with Bornhuetter Hall, we chose to terminate the monumental limestone face at an informal public seat, bringing together the need for a residential dorm to both reflect the value of the college and its serious educational mission, while acknowledging the students for whom the residence hall is a private place. The shape of the Nazareth House is generated through a negotiation between aesthetic code requirements that call for a conventional pitched suburban form in the front and opportunities of the site that are best exploited through an expansive glass pavilion at the rear, resulting in a continually deformed roof that opportunistically morphs between these competing demands (see Tactic: Paradoxical Pleasures, p. 172).

Identifying unresolved tensions and inherent paradoxes of culture often intentionally involves a sense of humor or wit. In this sense, wit is the creative act of acknowledging double binds or incompatible positions occupying the same space or location. Humor enables a project to speak to multiple audiences or users, acknowledging all parties in locating unintentional meanings or misinterpretations that arise out of contested expectations. In architecture, this means bringing to the foreground these moments of contestation, which in turn enables a project to be self-critical of the conditions that frame it while remaining engaged in the process, thus avoiding cynicism or the debilitating aspects of irony. In the case of the restaurant Lozoo, the limited space available for restrooms meant we did not have the luxury of providing separate men's and women's areas. Instead, we separated the water closets into individual rooms, while maintaining a shared space for the sinks, creating a situation that would heighten the theatrical social event caused by combining genders in a confined and typically private space. To intensify this condition, we unified the sinks into a single sloping stainless-steel surface with three separate, custom mirrors designating the individual washing and primping locations and integrated the water spout into these mirrors, such that the water poured down their surfaces. Cleaning one's hands meant the water obscures a view of one's face, creating, in effect, an updated restaging of the myth of Narcissus within the confines of a modern restaurant.

In the wallcovering design for Knoll Textiles, *Parallel Lines*, created through a combination of hand drawing and digitally generated repetition, we take pleasure in the idea that installing the covering means doing the one thing that all parents tell

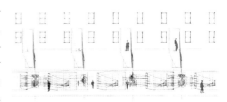

Exquisite Corpse Clothing Store
Following the logic of the fashion industry's division of the body, this proposed store is broken into four linked shops: shoes, pants, shirts/jackets, hats. Each is accessed through a 30'-wide revolving door. One can enter the door and not enter the store. The signs above the street double as catwalk-like changing rooms, designed to test public reaction to potential purchases.

their children not to do—draw on the wall. Our pursuit of multivalent performance often leads to an architecture of audacity where fluorescent light bulbs float in water (Water + Architecture); where the walls of a coffee shop are made from the same materials as a coffee cup (Ini Ani); where one drives home to the top of a skyscraper (Park Tower); where a mosaic of air fresheners map out a car in section in a city without automobiles—Venice (Parking Sections); where suburban houses grow on the roofs of sprawling commercial strip malls (New Suburbanism); and where pools of water are cantilevered beyond the face of a building, forty stories above a desert floor (Vegas 888).

At a time in which technologies of social, interpersonal isolation are multiplying—witness the recent growth of home-entertainment rooms and the decline in movie attendance—we are particularly interested in the critical role an architecture of multivalent performance can play in intensifying everyday public experiences through overlapping functions and creative juxtapositions. The majority of the projects that we take on are public in nature, as we have intentionally focused our time on works that can be visited and engaged, including restaurants, institutional buildings, and speculative projects exhibited in public museums. We take pleasure in transforming even small spaces at street level—some under 500 square feet—into destinations for everyday use. On a larger urban scale, we maintain that architecture can effectively short-circuit current directions of urban growth and land-use patterns through an examination of the underlying economic conditions and technologies that have shaped and formed these patterns. For the project New Suburbanism this means a reexamination of the interdependence between the big box store and the current growth of the mini-mansion. By finding their redundancies, we offer an alternative possibility that upholds the spatial independence that makes suburban houses attractive and the big boxes economically efficient, while cutting away at the excessive horizontal sprawl, thus producing extraordinary efficiencies of time, energy, and spatial organization. Park Tower anticipates a potential future where hydrogen vehicles will allow the suburban car culture to flourish within a dense urban city block: a drive-up, mixed-use skyscraper.

We are interested in an architecture that multiplies the contingent experiences of life, challenging the tendency toward increased specialization and insulation. We maintain that a successful project performs or operates on many, often incompatible, levels, holding in tension contradictory demands and celebrating productive paradoxes. Rather than supporting a singular ideological posture, we are interested in an architecture of nuance, play, and wit. By this, we engage the built environment, transforming limits into catalysts for invention where a combination of critical and speculative desires merge to construct opportunistic architecture.

New York, January 2007

Eavesdropping

This installation explores the most interesting sound in a gallery—the conversation overheard. A microphone eavesdrops on the gallery, relaying sounds to a series of speakers in front of ten chairs. When closed, the chairs form a corridor for listening adjacent to the speaker. When open, the 12'-high chairs masquerade as sculpture.

Arthouse at the Jones Center

Austin, Texas

Located in the heart of downtown Austin, this project is a renovation and expansion of an existing contemporary art space. LTL was commissioned to design 14,000 square feet of new program within the building envelope, including an entry lounge, a video/projects room, a large open gallery, multipurpose room, two artists' studios, additional art preparation areas, and an occupiable roof deck.

The existing building is an idiosyncratic hybrid of a 1920s theater and a 1950s department store. The architecture is pulled in two directions—as a theater its focus was on the stage, at the west, while as a store it was oriented to the street, at the east. The building's structure is both a concrete frame with steel trusses and, contained within the concrete frame, a single-story steel frame with a concrete deck. The theater's single large proscenium space was cut in half by the department store's second-floor addition.

LTL sought to intensify this peculiar accumulation of history by conceiving of the design as a series of integrated tactical additions and adjustments. These supplements revive and augment existing features—such as the 1920s trusses, concrete frame, and ornamental painting and the 1950s awning, storefront, and upper-level display window. The design will also open the second floor and roof through new vertical circulation and, most importantly, efficiently add program spaces and objects that allow the building to function and to have a presence in the city as a contemporary art institution. The elevation is perforated by 162 laminated glass blocks. Aggregated where light is needed on the interior, these apertures unify the building and form a logical yet unconventional facade appropriate for an experimental art venue.

Concrete frame with steel trusses

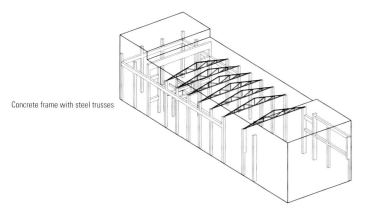

Queen Theatre, 1926

Steel frame with concrete floor

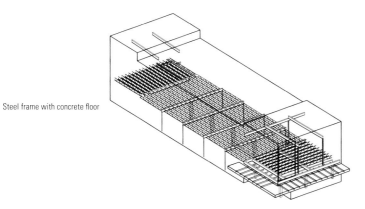

Lerner Shops, 1956

Two artists' studios

Photovoltaic panels

Roof deck

Mechanical

Stair and elevator

Mobile gallery wall

Screening

Awning

Central stair

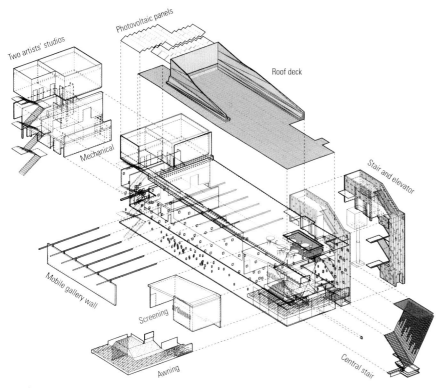

Tactical adjustments

Arthouse, 2004

Entry lounge

The original department store display window is enlarged to match the 640 x 480 pixel ratio proportions of video. This large opening of the second-floor multipurpose room doubles as a projection screen visible from the street at night.

The entry lounge is wrapped in floor-to-ceiling glass, maximizing sidewalk exposure and allowing glimpses beyond the reception desk into both levels of galleries.

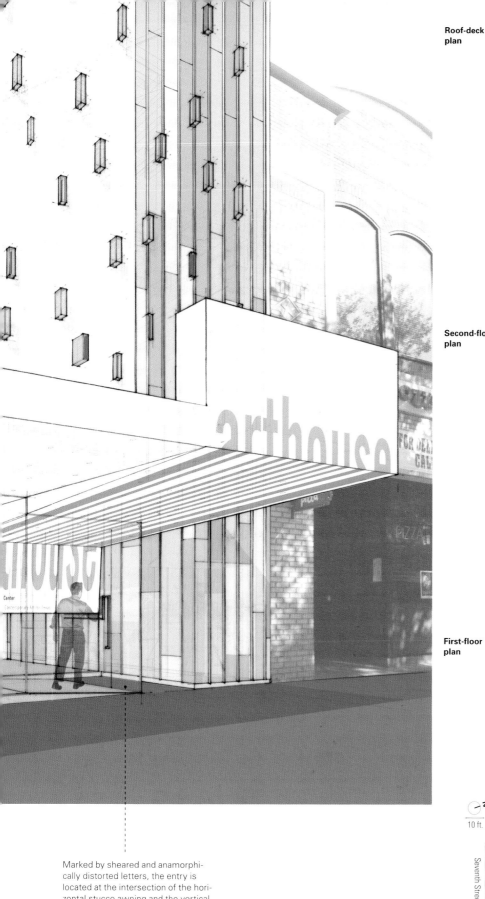

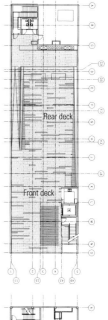

Roof-deck plan

Rear deck

Front deck

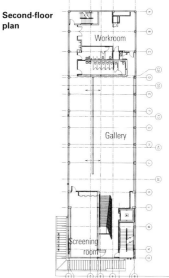

Second-floor plan

Workroom

Gallery

Screening room

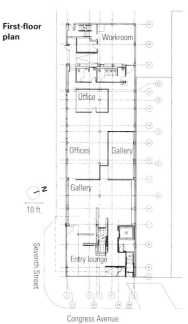

First-floor plan

Workroom

Office

Offices

Gallery

Gallery

10 ft.

Entry lounge

Seventh Street

Marked by sheared and anamorphically distorted letters, the entry is located at the intersection of the horizontal stucco awning and the vertical stainless-steel-clad stair tower. One enters Arthouse through its name.

Congress Avenue

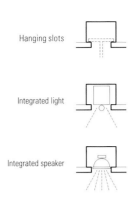

Hanging slots

Integrated light

Integrated speaker

The awning is perforated with three types of circular devices: anchor holes for suspending both artwork and exhibition signage, lights for both interior and sidewalk illumination, and speakers for audio projects, audible both within the lobby and on the outside. These perforations are randomly yet evenly dispersed at the sidewalk and increase in density and regularity toward the wall behind the reception desk.

The stucco awning, added during the department store conversion, is put on functional steroids. In addition to providing shade and capturing sidewalk territory, the awning extends into the building, further enhancing its ability to integrate the street and gallery. Vertical tabs, both up and down, added at the entry, provide the surface of the Arthouse sign. As a sculptural ceiling, the awning defines distinct areas in the entry lounge and forms the wall at the back of the reception desk.

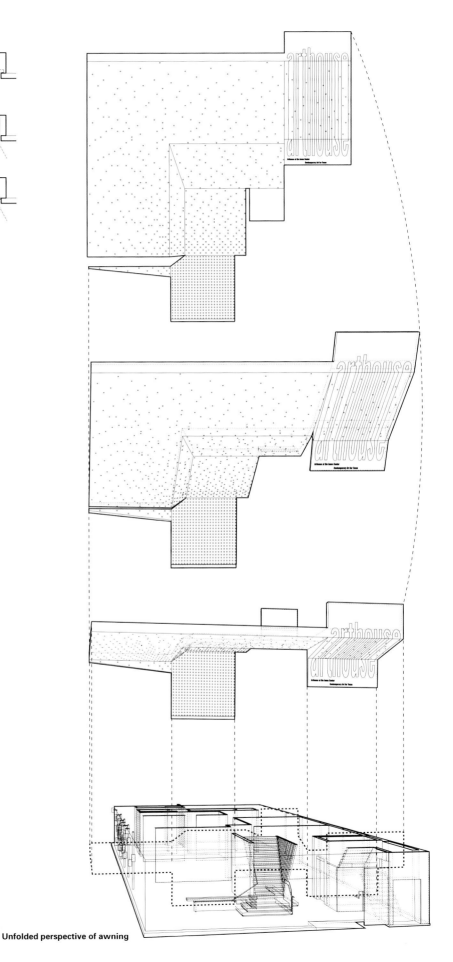

Unfolded perspective of awning

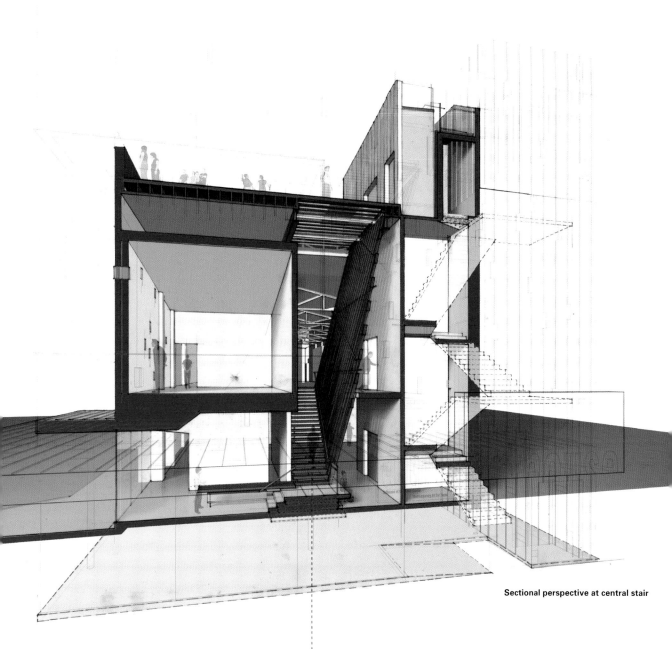

Sectional perspective at central stair

Entry lounge and central stair

The central stair provides the primary spatial connection to the main second-floor gallery. Its lower portion is made of stacked precast concrete planks, while the upper portion is suspended from the wooden roof deck. In a sense, one ascends from the ground onto the roof while remaining within the gallery. The first wood tread becomes the reception desk, while the concrete planks provide areas of repose. The staircase is both playful and grand, weightless and grounded, expansive and local.

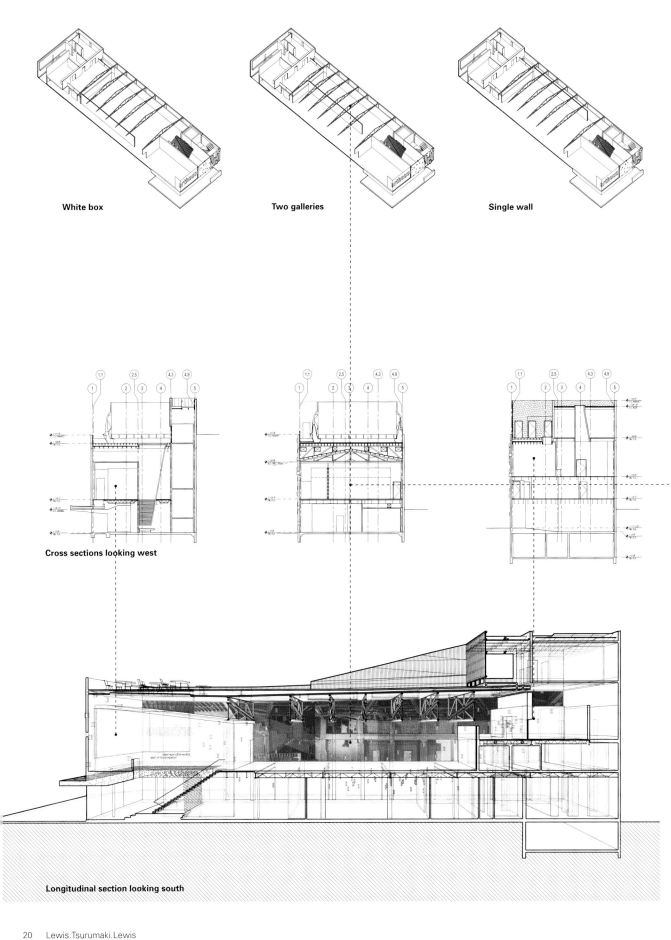

White box

Two galleries

Single wall

Cross sections looking west

Longitudinal section looking south

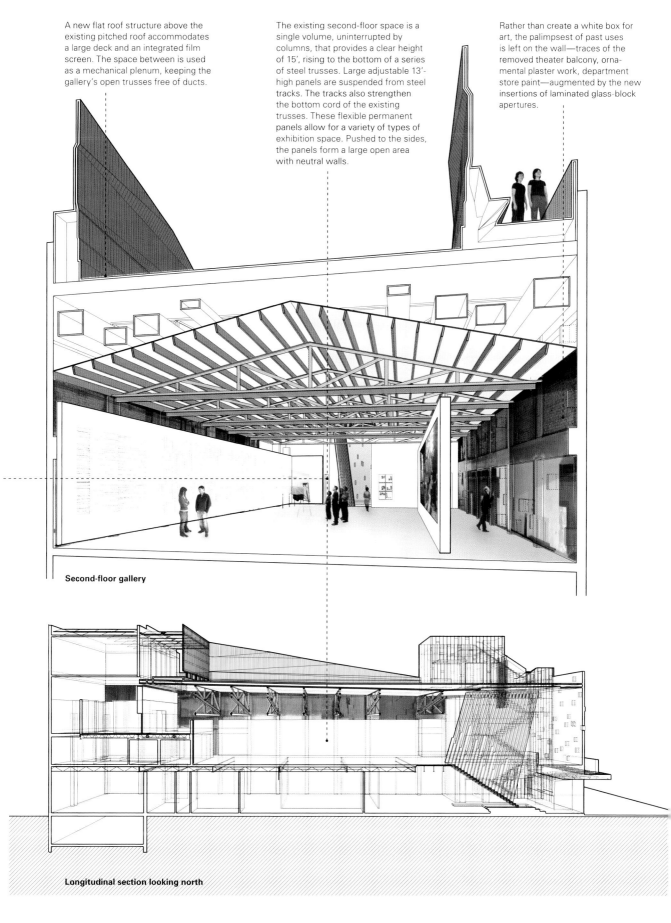

A new flat roof structure above the existing pitched roof accommodates a large deck and an integrated film screen. The space between is used as a mechanical plenum, keeping the gallery's open trusses free of ducts.

The existing second-floor space is a single volume, uninterrupted by columns, that provides a clear height of 15', rising to the bottom of a series of steel trusses. Large adjustable 13'-high panels are suspended from steel tracks. The tracks also strengthen the bottom cord of the existing trusses. These flexible permanent panels allow for a variety of types of exhibition space. Pushed to the sides, the panels form a large open area with neutral walls.

Rather than create a white box for art, the palimpsest of past uses is left on the wall—traces of the removed theater balcony, ornamental plaster work, department store paint—augmented by the new insertions of laminated glass-block apertures.

Second-floor gallery

Longitudinal section looking north

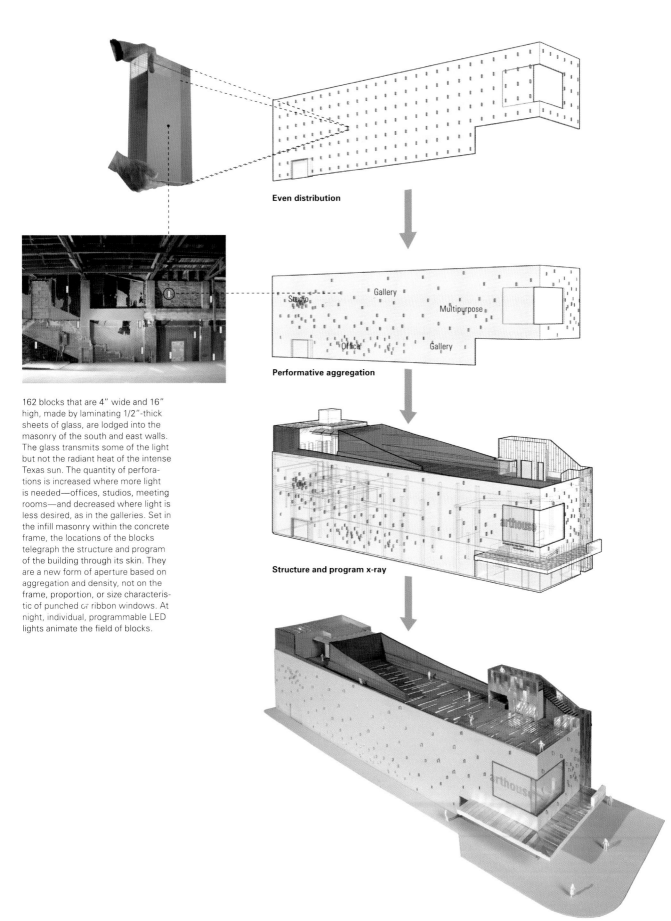

Even distribution

Performative aggregation

Studio   Gallery

Office   Multipurpose

Gallery

Structure and program x-ray

162 blocks that are 4" wide and 16" high, made by laminating 1/2"-thick sheets of glass, are lodged into the masonry of the south and east walls. The glass transmits some of the light but not the radiant heat of the intense Texas sun. The quantity of perforations is increased where more light is needed—offices, studios, meeting rooms—and decreased where light is less desired, as in the galleries. Set in the infill masonry within the concrete frame, the locations of the blocks telegraph the structure and program of the building through its skin. They are a new form of aperture based on aggregation and density, not on the frame, proportion, or size characteristic of punched or ribbon windows. At night, individual, programmable LED lights animate the field of blocks.

Roof deck

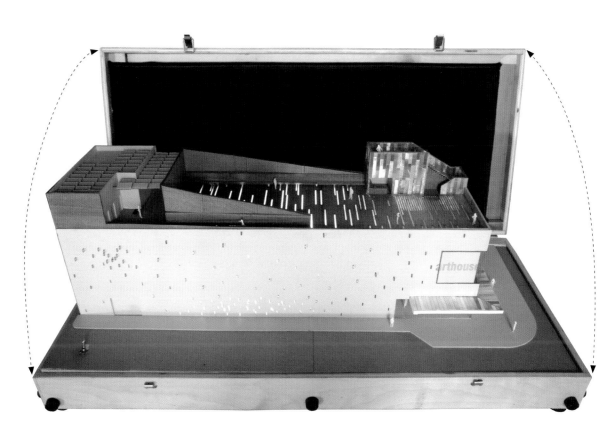

Illuminated model in portable display case

Bornhuetter Hall

Wooster, Ohio

This project for the College of Wooster began in 2001 with an extensive feasibility study of the residential campus plan that culminated in recommendations for substantial changes in the density and configuration of several student halls. Contrary to the prevailing trend at residential colleges toward apartment-style living, extensive discussions with students, residential-life staff, and the college's administration led to the unanticipated conclusion that a double-loaded corridor typology actually encourages the greatest degree of socialization and the most positive student experiences. Urban where the apartment type is suburban, the spatial format of the corridor building facilitates exchange among students and provides opportunities for diverse levels of interaction. At a time when students arrive on campus with an increasing array of insulating personal technologies—iPods, computers, Game Boys—this seemingly outmoded housing type offers a social mixing chamber for the cultivation of a collective collegial identity.

The success of the double-loaded corridor as a catalyst for college social life is predicated on several important conditions: 1) the scale of the hall unit—the total number of rooms served by a single corridor—should be neither too small nor too large, as this results either in isolation or institutional anonymity, 2) the corridor should be wide enough to function as an ad-hoc social space and connect to or incorporate other collective spaces, and 3) the corridor should be integrated with the main circulation paths through the building.

The generative brief for Bornhuetter Hall, a new 47,500-square-foot residence hall with 185 beds, was partially derived through this research. Sited on the northern edge of a liberal-arts campus, Bornhuetter Hall encourages social interaction by transforming the conventions of the double-loaded corridor and enriches student experience by providing a balance between private spaces for study and public gathering areas for communal life and discussion.

The spatial diagram for the building is the product of resolving conflicting pressures. The college requested a single building not to exceed four floors. Therefore, each floor needed to hold forty-six students, yet according to the research, the ideal hall unit should be limited to twenty-five to thirty students.

To solve this dilemma, the building was split into two parts, connected by an exterior courtyard. The existing site features—a parking lot and a pine grove—determined the different lengths of each portion of the building. By extending the brick and glass skins of the building around the courtyard, the two residence halls appear to be a single building. Within each wing, the hallways flare at their ends and embrace lounges, a kitchenette, and more intimate sitting areas. A collective outdoor courtyard is created by this split, and this exterior room functions as the public center of the building. It is an unusual space, simultaneously at the heart of the building and at the ends of each wing, containing both social and private spaces. It provides a sequence of entry into the building and a passage from the campus to the park beyond.

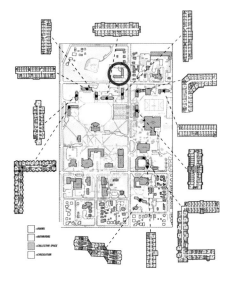

Campus plan and existing residence halls

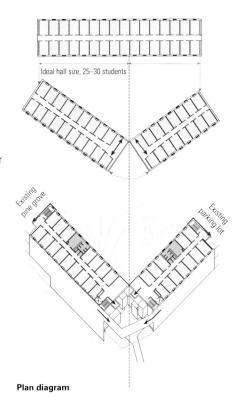

Ideal hall size, 25–30 students

Existing pine grove

Existing parking lot

Plan diagram

Second- and third-floor plan

First-floor plan

Ground-floor plan

10 ft.

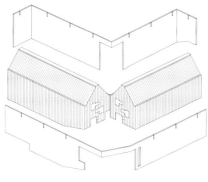

The hall is sited at the northern edge of the campus adjacent to a park with ballfields. The courtyard both provides the major collective space for the building and forms a link between the campus and the landscape beyond. One can move through the building to the park—from outside to outside—without passing through a door.

The building is conceived as two copper-clad boxes wrapped by two veneers of brick. The brick skins unify the building, while the details at the corners, windows, and joints of the building explicate the interplay between the brick surfaces and the copper volume.

Wood-clad study nooks cantilever, like box seats, into the theatrical space of the courtyard, producing a dynamic entrance to the building and establishing private study areas in a collective setting. The daily activity of coming and going from the residence hall becomes a public event.

The courtyard is sh
of channel glas
for a dynamic an
to the exterior. F
the building, th
produce a consta
of transparency. T
of the glass col
views betweer
the entry walkwa
the views to anc
on the adjacent
screen animate
sunlight and shado
and provides a veil

LTL's design capitalizes on the opportunities and paradoxes of conventional systems of construction. The brick facades are treated as independent planes sheathing internal volumes clad in copper—an approach that reflects the veneer nature of the cavity wall construction. The layering and interplay between the brick skins and the copper volume is most evident at the ends of the building. Copper awnings, installed on the public, campus sides of the building to provide shading and depth, are treated as extensions of the interior volume through the openings of the brick skin. At the front, the formal limestone frame at the entry is extended down to form a side entry and a seat, playfully linking the monumental and the prosaic.

Pre-cast concrete plank proved a cost-effective and rapid means to construct the floors. It also provided an opportunity to alleviate the potential blandness of the stacked corridors by introducing a gap between the planks cantilevered from the bearing walls of the rooms over the corridor. The resulting slot houses recessed hallway lighting, introducing vertical articulation into an otherwise flat ceiling. Carpet was continued up the wall of the hallways to encourage social loitering. Located on the ground floor, a larger multi-purpose room, wrapped in bamboo, connects directly to the park.

The communal lounges allow for contrasting views of the park and campus. On one side, an expansive glass wall opens to a serene park landscape of pines and grass while the study nooks provide more selective, active vantage points toward the courtyard and campus.

Overlooking the interior courtyard, the study nooks are sized for individual or small-group study. In this way, the coming together of two or three students is also the moment of contact with the larger community of the residence hall. From within the perch of the study nooks, students can see the activity in adjacent nooks, the comings and goings in the courtyard below, and the campus and street activity beyond the channel-glass screen. The study nooks' proximity to hall traffic and lounge activity means that students can both withdraw and engage in the community at the same time.

Since the lounges mirror each other
across the interior corner of the
L-shaped plan, it is possible to look
from one lounge into another,
allowing for visual contact between
physically separated halls and levels.

Building 82%

Miami Beach, Florida

Providing an alternative to the glut of high-end condo towers in Miami Beach—typically hermetic, single-use structures sealed off from any relation to context or climate—the design for Building 82% intensifies urban, programmatic, and spatial permeability. Exploiting the desirability of outdoor space in South Florida, the designs for the project amplify the possibilities of regional architectural strategies—balconies, terraces, atria, courtyards, and breezeways—by recombining them in unexpected ways to maximize the connections between interior and exterior space. Specifically, the design opportunistically manipulates the fact that only eighty-two percent of the available zoning volume for the site could be filled with built volume according to the floor area ratio (FAR) limits. Rather than locate this extra volume as a private interior courtyard, the extra volume is located around the public exterior, producing an undulating elevation with depth and greater variety of interior views. In a sense, Le Corbusier's Dom-ino diagram is eaten away by the free plan and free facade.

Reflecting its position at the border between a commercial zone and the residential neighborhoods to its west, the project incorporates retail, parking, and live-work spaces. While in most mixed-use projects programmatic zones are indifferently stacked one on the other, LTL's design creates overlaps and interdependencies between its component parts. Thus the commercial plinth of the building is created as a synthetic "landscape," a new ground for the residential units above, allowing for the introduction of exterior green space. Vertical connections facilitate integration between levels and uses, with the plinth acting as a meeting ground between public and private, commercial and domestic space.

The principal design challenge was the relationship between the units and the exterior spaces they defined. Various schemes—split bar, L-shape, and three bar—were considered that negotiated differing typologies of exterior space, relationships between living and working, economies of construction, and market forces determining unit sizes and numbers. Over the course of the design process, the pressures of a declining real estate market required revisions for greater density, increasing unit counts, and limiting the amount of exterior space that could be maintained. In the end, open space remains the greatest luxury in Miami.

Split bar

Total FAR	23,950 sq. ft.
Max FAR	44,904 sq. ft.
Density	0.53

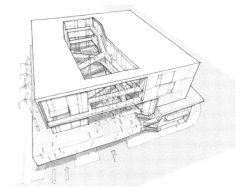

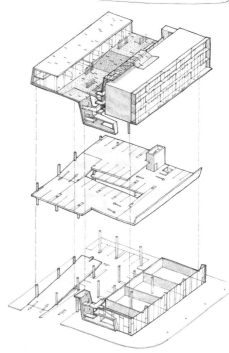

Miami

Miami Beach

L-shape

Total FAR	27,400 sq. ft.
Max FAR	44,904 sq. ft.
Density	0.61

Three bar

Total FAR	35,700 sq. ft.
Max FAR	44,904 sq. ft.
Density	0.79

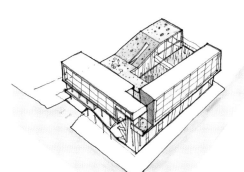

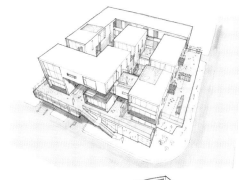

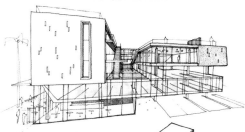

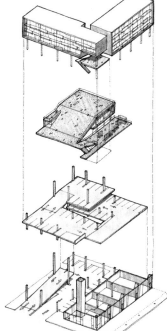

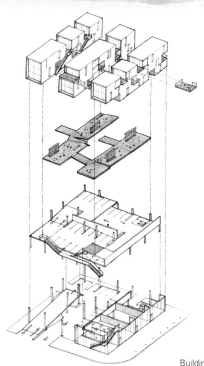

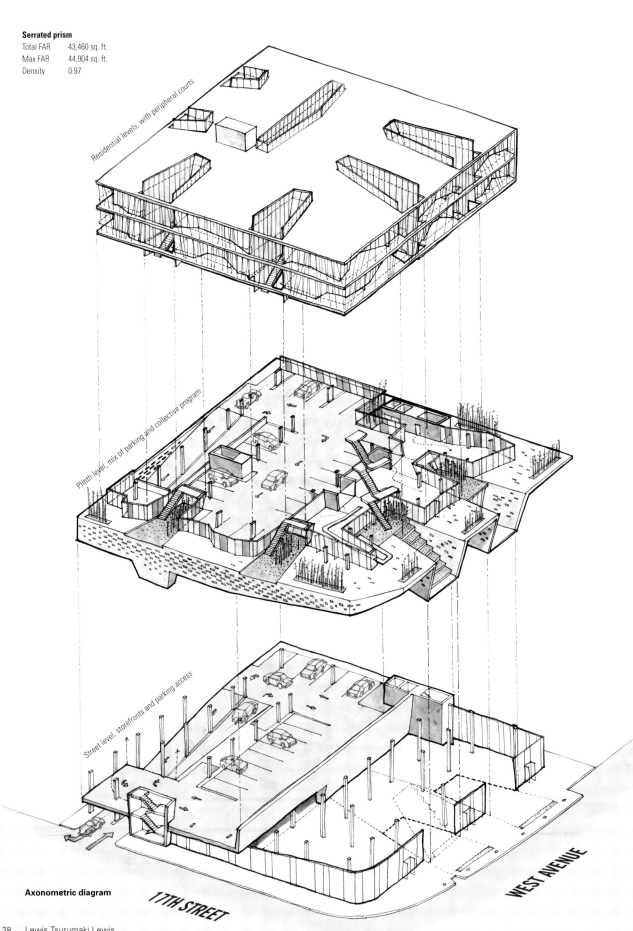

Serrated prism

Total FAR	43,460 sq. ft.
Max FAR	44,904 sq. ft.
Density	0.97

Residential levels, with peripheral courts

Plinth level, mix of parking and collective program

Street level, storefronts and parking access

Axonometric diagram

17TH STREET

WEST AVENUE

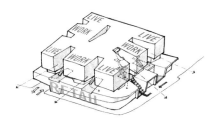

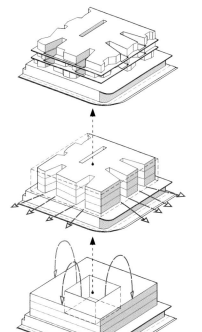

Sequential diagram

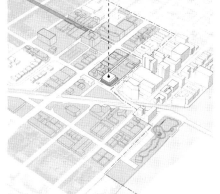

Site

4.
Miami code allows a 5' zone around the building's perimeter. The slabs of each floor plate extend to this legal limit, producing a continuous exterior terrace. Undulations in the glazing envelope generate variation in dimension, forming a series of outdoor rooms, while the vertical courts provide property divisions between units.

3.
The extra volume forms a series of vertical cuts in the facade, choreographed to increase light to and views from the building.

2.
Rather than place the extra volume in an interior courtyard, the 18% is moved to the public face.

1.
The maximum FAR, with standard ceiling heights, filled 82% of the maximum building volume.

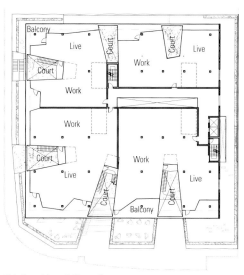

Third- and fourth-floor plan

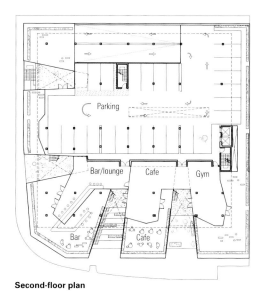

Second-floor plan

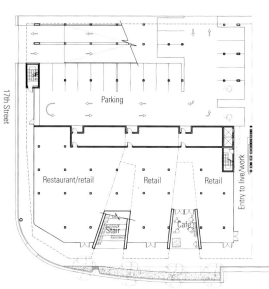

First-floor plan   West Avenue

The building comprises a commercial plinth surmounted by a volume of live-work residential units. Exploiting the possibilities of this programmatic stacking, the plinth is transformed into a new ground, an elevated tropical landscape for the residential units above. It also acts as a shared territory where residents and the public commingle.

The surface of the plinth folds down along the pedestrian walkway, producing an undulating ribbon of concrete that forms storefronts and interiors, integrating them with alternating exterior circulation, dining, and seating areas. In effect, the space of the street dovetails into the retail frontages.

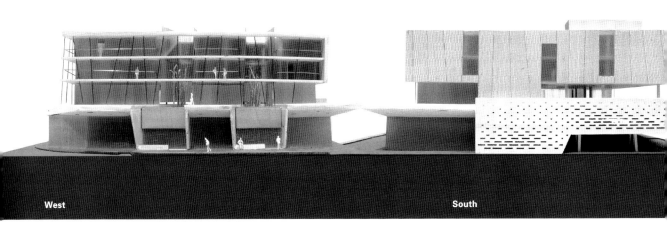

West

South

The balcony rail is formed by a veil of vertical steel strands tensioned between the horizontal floor slabs. Below, the cables are arrayed to satisfy the code limits of spacing, intermittently extending vertically to suspend the rail, creating a visually fluctuating perimeter.

Whereas the loft-like live/work volume is planar in articulation, the plinth is conceived as a solid permeated with light and exterior space. The plasticity of concrete is employed to generate contrasting spatial effects—from the thin edges of the residential slabs to the thickened surfaces of the commercial base.

Pirating the traditions of Miami Modernism, the retail and parking plinth is perforated by a system of variable openings that operate like an enlarged version of a screen block wall. The size and density of the perforation is generated by the ventilation requirements of the enclosed parking garage. The resulting perforation patterns create shifting views that are calibrated to the movement of passing pedestrians and cars.

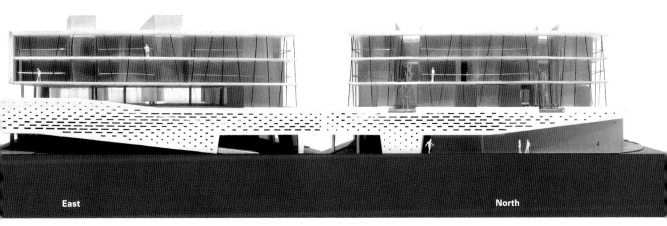

East

North

Interior of live/work unit

Sectional perspective of court and urban stair

Perimeter courtyards carve inward from the building edge, producing multi-level atria that establish property divisions among balconies, define living and working zones within units, and create visual connections between the residential volume, the plinth, and the street. Variable translucencies in the window wall provide privacy and limit visual access between units. Stairs located within each court provide circulation from the lofts to the gardens below. Near the major street corner, an over-scaled urban stair folds down to connect the plinth to the street to the elevated landscape and residential units.

Skin studies

Dash Dogs

New York, New York

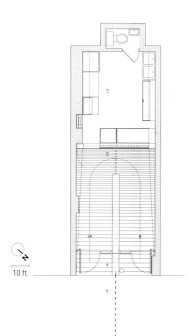

Dash Dogs is located in the Lower East Side of New York City. LTL's design for this 220-square-foot hot-dog stand paradoxically makes the small space smaller in order to produce the illusion of a larger space. The ceiling slopes down two feet, while the floor slopes up six inches from the sidewalk storefront entry, thereby creating a forced perspective. The sloping surfaces of the steel wrapper converge at the sales counter to imply depth and continuity within a space that is only twice as long as it is wide. The project formalizes the literal sequence of take-out, leading the customer from the sidewalk to the grill, the cash register, eating counter, and back to the sidewalk. The division between coming in and going out becomes an architectural feature; embedded lights lodged in the gaps between the steel wrapper form a dotted line along the axis. Located at the division between entry and exit, a laminated bamboo plywood counter is cantilevered twelve feet through the glass storefront. Inside, the counter floats within the space and provides a horizontal datum against which to read the slope of the floor and ceiling.

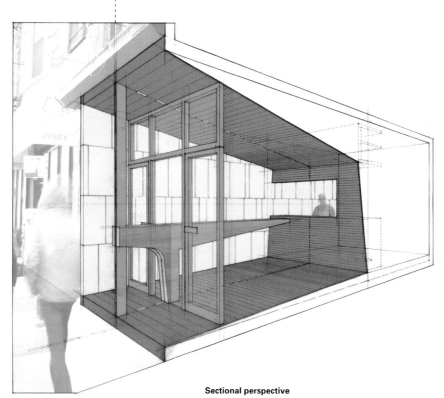

Sectional perspective

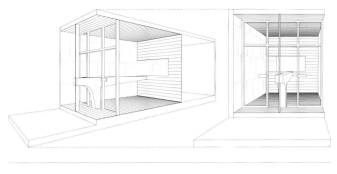

Diagram of flat floor and ceiling

A technique typically deployed in Baroque theaters, palace staircases, and film sets, forced perspective here enhances a hot-dog stand. The space appears deeper, the hot dogs longer and bigger.

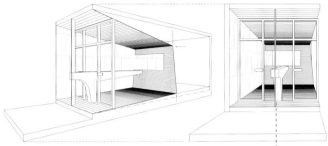

Diagram of sloped floor and ceiling

The surface of the floors, counter, and ceiling is made of 1/8"-thick bars of blackened hot-rolled steel. The width of the bars varies from 6" wide at the street to 2" at the counter to accentuate the forced perspective illusion. Likewise, the illuminated gaps between every other band produce a diminishing dashed line. Randomly drilled countersunk stainless steel screws constitute a field pattern that animates the steel surface.

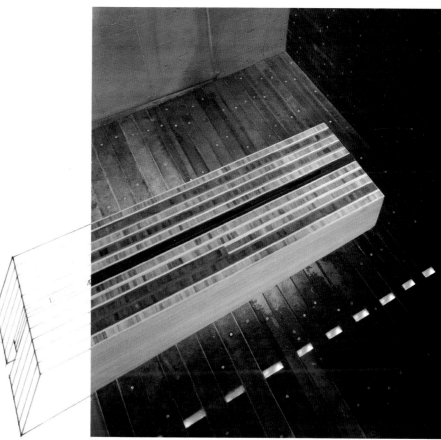

3/4" bamboo-plywood sheets are layered together to form an 8"-thick eating counter. The horizontal counter and the sloped floor provide different eating heights down the length of the space. The side walls are sealed concrete panels cut into random 3' vertical strips. Its rough quality is in direct contrast with the crisp steel wrapper and precise bamboo counter.

Display Devices
Various Galleries

Light Structures (wall version) uses 4' fluorescent lightbulbs suspended by cables as the structure for backlit image displays. Like the floor version, this exhibit can be easily shipped, without bulbs, to a new location.

Light Structures (floor version) uses 8' fluorescent lightbulbs as the structure for holding backlit images. The electrical ballast doubles as the weight at the base. This exhibit was first displayed at the University of Texas in Austin.

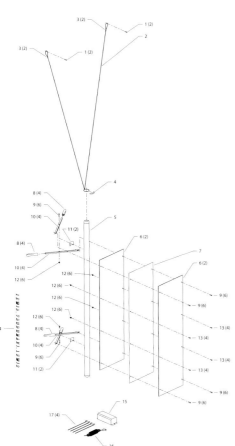

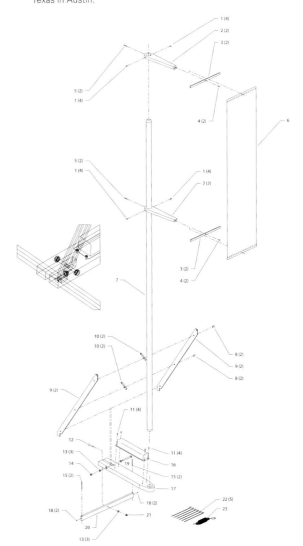

1. #10 Stainless Steel Wood Screw (2)
2. 1/16" Stainless Steel Wire Rope
3. 13/64" O.D. Zinc-Plated Copper Compression Sleeve (2)
4. 1/32" Black Rubber
5. 48" T12 Linear Fluorescent Bulb, Double-Pin Base
6. 0.060" Thick, 10" x 34" Clear Acrylic (2)
7. 10" x 34" Back-Lite Film
8. 1/4" x 3/4" x 4 3/4" Foam Grip (4)
9. #10-24, 5/8" Stainless Steel Socket Cap Screw (6)
10. 3/8" x 1/4" Steel Bar (4)
11. 1/32" Transparent Rubber
12. #10-24 Stainless Steel Hex Nut (6)
13. #10-24, 3/8" Stainless Steel Socket Cap Screw (4)
14. Peel-and-Stick Vinyl Lettering
15. Rapid Start Fluorescent Ballast
16. 18 GA Black Electrical Cord
17. 8" White Nylon Cable Tie (4)

1. 3/4" Nylon Set Screw (4)
2. 3/4" Stained Birch Plywood (2)
3. 1/2" x 1/4" Steel Bar (2)
4. #8 Stainless Steel Wood Screw (2)
5. 1/8" Diameter Steel Rod (2)
6. 12" x 48" Back-Lite Film
7. 96" T12 Linear Fluorescent Bulb, Single-Pin Base
8. 1/4"-20 Stainless Steel Machine Screw (2)
9. 3/16" x 1-1/2" Steel Bar (2)
10. 3/8" x 1/4" Steel Bar (2)
11. #8 Black-Oxide Wood Screw (4)
12. 1/4"-20 Stainless Steel Socket Cap Screw
13. 0.688" Diameter Steel Washer (3)
14. 5/16"-18 Steel Hex Nut
15. 5/16" Steel Rod (2)
16. Rapid Start Fluorescent Ballast
17. 1-1/8" Stained Birch Plywood
18. 1/4"-20 Steel Set Screw (2)
19. 5/16"-18 Steel Hex Head Bolt
20. 1-1/4" x 1/2" Steel Bar
21. 1/4"-20 Steel Hex Nut
22. 8" Black Nylon Cable Tie (5)
23. 18 GA Black Electrical Cord

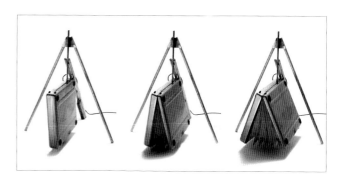

Water Vitrines, used in the exhibition Architecture + Water, float a fluorescent light bulb in a 6″ x 6″ x 6′ acrylic box half filled with water. The box is balanced on a steel and wood base, and image panels are adhered to the fronts. The vitrines are linked by hoses, producing a single flat water level.

For the Voting Booth Project from 2004, participants each received an original Votomatic booth from Florida—decommissioned after the 2000 election—which they were to imaginatively redesign. LTL's project, entitled *Bellow*, imagined the booth in a state of animated exhaustion, where the case continuously opens and closes, accompanied by recorded sounds of belabored breathing.

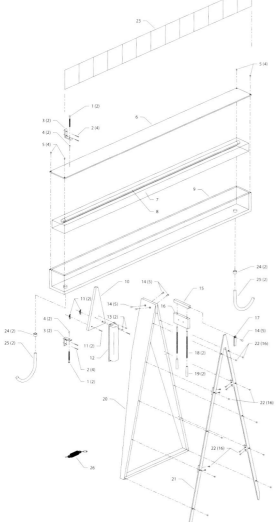

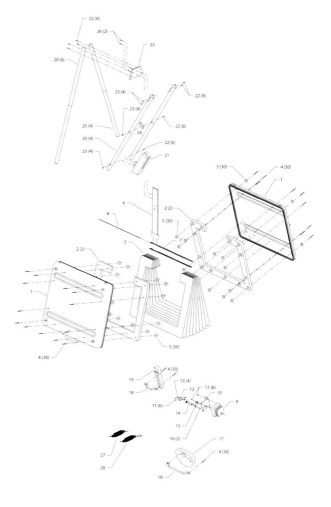

1. 1/4″-20, 3 1/2″ Thumb Screw (2)
2. #10 Stainless Steel Wood Screw (4)
3. 2 1/2″ x 2 1/2″ x 1/4″ Steel Angle (2)
4. Red Polyethylene Cap (2)
5. #8 Stainless Steel Machine Screw (4)
6. 1/2″ Thick Clear Acrylic Lid
7. Water
8. 72″ T12 Linear Fluorescent Bulb with End Caps
9. 6″ x 6″ x 72″, 1/2″ Thick Clear Acrylic Box
10. 3/4″ Stained Birch Plywood
11. 1/4″-20 Stainless Steel Wall Anchor (2)
12. Rapid Start Fluorescent Ballast
13. #8 Stainless Steel Wood Screw (2)
14. #10 Stainless Steel Machine Screw (5)
15. 1″ x 1″ Steel Bar
16. 1″ x 4″ Steel Bar
17. 1″ x 1/8″ Steel Bar
18. 1/4″ Threaded Rod (2)
19. 4 1/2″ Threaded Vinyl Grip (2)
20. 3/4″ Stained Birch Plywood
21. 1″ x 1/4″ Steel with Welded Tabs
22. #8 Stainless Steel Machine Screw (16)
23. 6″ x 72″ Back-Lite Film
24. 1/2″ Tube Fitting (2)
25. 1/2″ Dia. Clear Neoprene Tubing (2)
26. 18 GA Black Electrical Cord

1. Aluminum Votomatic Case
2. 3/4″ Plywood Mounting Panel (2)
3. Sewn Neoprene Coated Nylon Bellows
4. 3/16″ Dia. Aluminum Blind Rivet (30)
5. 1″ Dia. Zinc-Coated Steel Washer (30)
6. 2″ x 1/4″ Steel Bar
7. Stainless Steel Piano Hinge
8. 1/16″ Dia. Steel Rod
9. Worm Gear Motor
10. 1/16″ Formed Aluminum Bracket
11. #8 Round Head Stainless Steel Machine Screw (6)
12. 1/16″ Formed Aluminum Mount
13. #8 Stainless Steel Hex Nut (4)
14. 1/8″ Shaped Steel Articulating Rod
15. 1/4″ Shaped Steel Master Rod
16. 1/4″-20 Stainless Steel Hex Head Machine Screw (2)
17. Digital Answering Machine
18. 3/4″ Punched Steel Strapping
19. Outlet Strip
20. Two-Part Votomatic Aluminum Legs (4)
21. 2″ x 3/4″ Steel Counterweight
22. 1/4″-20 Stainless Steel Pan Head Machine Screw (8)
23. 1/4″-20 Stainless Steel Hex Nut (4)
24. 2″ x 1/4″ Steel Bar
25. 3″ x 1/4″ Steel Bar
26. 1/4″-20 Stainless Steel Flat Head Machine Screw (2)
27. Coated Copper Wire
28. 18 GA Black Electrical Cord

Fluff Bakery

New York, New York

LTL's design for this 800-square-foot bakery and coffee shop fuses a highly efficient plan with an expressive surface that cloaks the walls and the ceiling. The plan provides the required space for the bakery and bathroom, maximizes the number of seats by locating booths in the storefront, and directs take-away traffic to the center. The storefront was recessed two feet from the property line to allow the entry to appear to extend into the sidewalk.

The attention of patrons is drawn immediately to the walls and ceiling, a robust surface made from layers of common materials. Almost 18,500 feet (more than three miles) of 3/4- by 3/4-inch strips of felt and stained plywood were individually positioned and anchored into place. The surface performs in multiple ways: as banquette back, as padding, as acoustic damper, and as visual seduction. The striking linear pattern of the strips induces a horizontal vertigo, which, seen through the glass storefront, serves as a visual attractor to pedestrians on the street. The vitality of this architectural surface becomes the shop's advertisement. As a counterpoint to the excessive linearity of the strips, a custom stainless-steel chandelier, composed of forty-two dimmable linear incandescent lights, branches across the ceiling.

Seductive surface

Efficient plan

In contrast to the illusion of movement and speed when viewed at an acute angle, the horizontal strips appear to flatten the space when seen straight on. In other words, when entering or exiting the space, the surface appears to intensify motion; yet, when sitting in the space, the surface effects a flat calm. The transition from wall to ceiling is hardly perceptible—an optical paradox.

The walls and ceiling are composed of specific combinations of three different types of industrial felt (F1, F7, F11) and three colors of stained Baltic birch plywood. The balance of grey, black, and white materials in the mixture is adjusted to produce a darker area at the seating areas to minimize the appearance of stains and wear, while lighter combinations fill the ceiling.

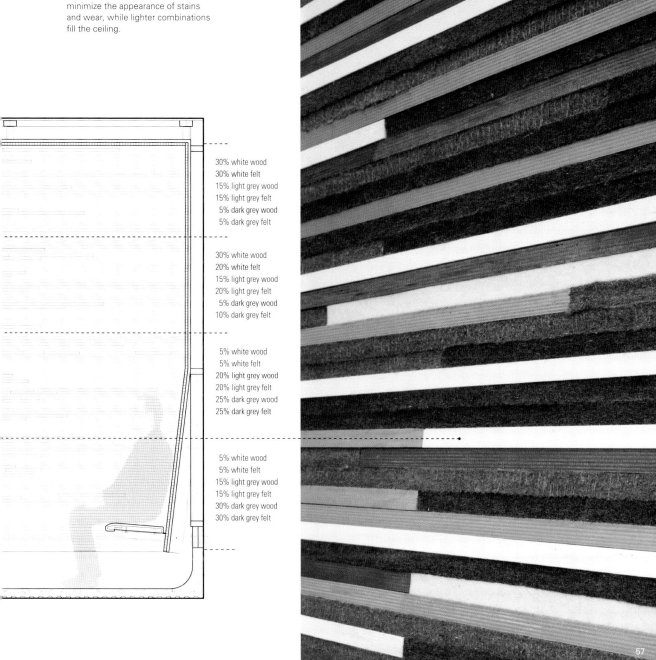

30% white wood
30% white felt
15% light grey wood
15% light grey felt
5% dark grey wood
5% dark grey felt

30% white wood
20% white felt
15% light grey wood
20% light grey felt
5% dark grey wood
10% dark grey felt

5% white wood
5% white felt
20% light grey wood
20% light grey felt
25% dark grey wood
25% dark grey felt

5% white wood
5% white felt
15% light grey wood
15% light grey felt
30% dark grey wood
30% dark grey felt

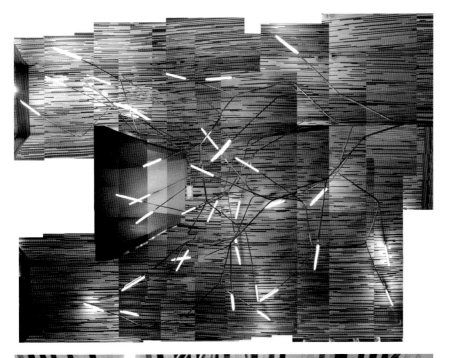

The horizontal chandelier explores the apparent randomness that can emerge from a limited set of parts. Forty-two 7'6" pieces of stainless-steel conduit are bent into just three types. Each type is assembled into ten branches. The middle bend of each unit is the splice point for the start of the next unit, while the end is connected to a linear incandescent bulb socket. The ten branches are anchored to a single steel spine located at the bottom of a fold in the ceiling surface and intertwined together within three feet of the ceiling. This rationally designed randomness distributes light evenly throughout the space.

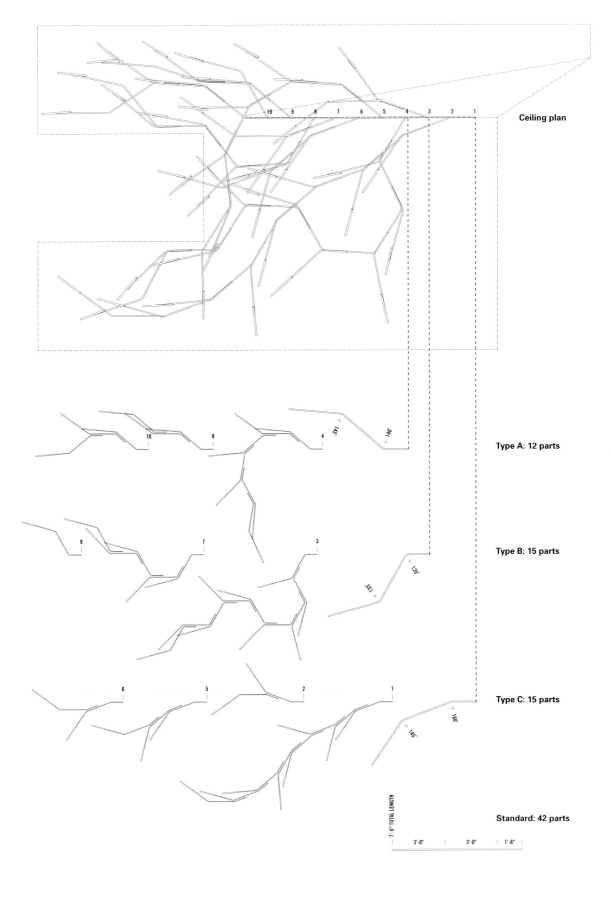

Ceiling plan

Type A: 12 parts

Type B: 15 parts

Type C: 15 parts

Standard: 42 parts

7'-6" TOTAL LENGTH

3'-0"   3'-0"   1'-6"

Four Exhibitions

Four Galleries, New York, New York

Recognizing that exhibition design must foreground content while using the idiosyncrasies of the gallery and the content to provoke inventive methods of display, LTL developed unique apparatuses and organizational systems for four exhibits. Two of the exhibits, Refiled and Architecture + Water, are based on thickening the gallery wall into a denser display apparatus, while FAAR-Out and Ten Shades of Green are predicated on the very lack of wall surface.

FAAR-Out

ADC Gallery, New York, NY
April–May 2003

This exhibition presented the work of twenty-nine Design Fellows from the American Academy in Rome. The large open exhibition hall at the ADG Gallery in New York City did not possess sufficient perimeter wall area to comfortably exhibit all the work. Therefore, temporary exhibition surface was added by suspending a fabric volume around each of the six columns in the center of the gallery. Each artist was given one side of the column volume, the width of their side set by the horizontal dimension required to exhibit their work. The resulting geometry of the enclosure and the space of the exhibition was a direct consequence of the size of the artists' work. The volumes were suspended, creating a floating datum line across the bottom of the exhibition, and lights located on the columns allowed the fabric volumes to glow. Hung with ropes and pulleys, the diaphanous volumes could be raised so that the space could be used as needed for other public functions.

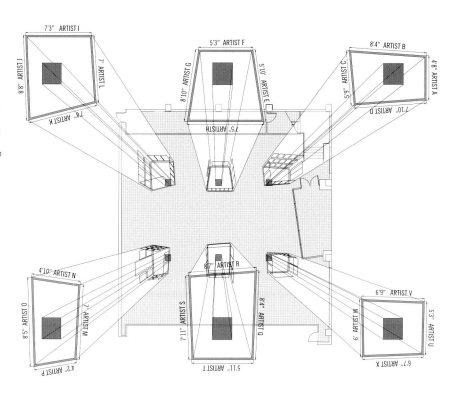

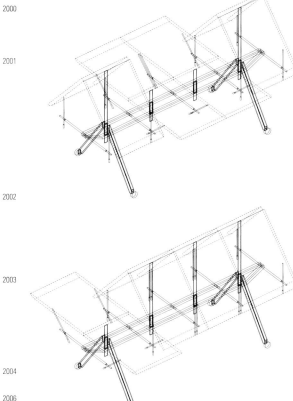

Ten Shades of Green

Architectural League of New York
The Urban Center, New York, NY
April–May 2000

LTL was invited by the Architectural League of New York to design the installation for a traveling exhibition presenting ten buildings from around the world that exemplified architectural innovations catalyzed by divergent approaches to sustainability. Deciding that each building should be displayed on a separate mobile table, LTL designed custom apparatuses composed of six, eight, or ten 3' x 2' plywood modules. Custom hardware allowed for adjustment to any position between horizontal and vertical in order to accommodate a variety of materials or equipment—models, drawings, photographs, or computers. For ease of travel, the modular components can be dismantled with a minimum of labor and the tables can be reconfigured according to the particular spatial restrictions of the respective venues. This exhibition has been shown in over fourteen different venues without the need for any new construction, temporary walls, or physical modifications. Because configuring it for a new venue requires no new materials, the exhibition's adaptability is its sustainability.

Architecture + Water

Van Alen Institute, New York, NY
March–September 2001
UCLA, Department of Architecture, Los Angeles, CA
November–December 2001
Heinz Architectural Center, Carnegie Museum of Art,
Pittsburgh, PA
February–May 2002
San Francisco Museum of Modern Art, San Francisco, CA
November 2002–February 2003

This exhibition was curated, designed, and built
by LTL for the Van Alen Institute in New York
City. Although typically conceived as opposites—
architecture is understood as fixed and stable,
while water is seen as fluid and dynamic—the
tension between these can provide constraints
and limitations that direct and inspire imaginative
architecture.

    The projects selected by LTL for this exhibi-
tion negotiate this contradiction. Rather than
relegating water to its conventional role as an
aesthetic feature, these projects directly incorporate water as a critical component in the orchestra-
tion of the design, celebrating water in its multiple
forms, as a functional, physical, and transformative
medium. Each project occupied an 18' wall wedged
out from the gallery wall to form a blackout space
for rear video projection. A continuous 1/2" hollow
acrylic tube, filled half full with water, formed a
literal level line down the gallery, aligning the
panels and organizing the graphic image display.

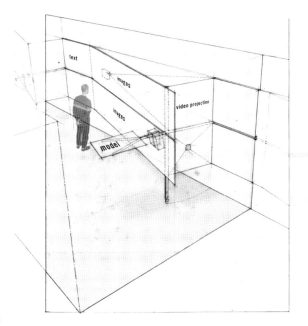

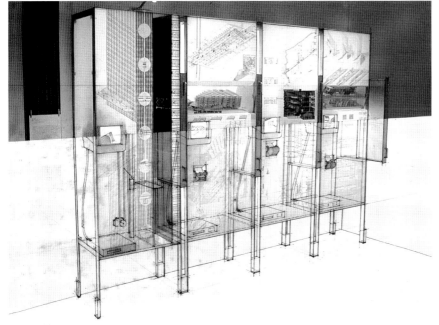

Refiled

The Cooper-Hewitt National Design Museum, New York, NY
March–August 2000

The installation Refiled was exhibited at the Cooper-Hewitt Museum in New York City in the first National Design Triennial in 2000, an overview of the leading developments in American architecture and design at the start of the new millennium. Asked to produce an installation under the general heading of "reclaimed," LTL designed and built a piece that plays upon outmoded systems of filing and classification. The installation was a hybrid of a light box, a cabinet of curiosities, and a storage filing system, reconfiguring all into an apparatus for display. Refiled was an installation in its own right, as well as a frame for displaying four projects: Mies-on-a-Beam, Tourbus Hotel, Sportbars, and New Suburbanism. Occupying the center of each 10'-high panel, a monitor displayed animations of each project. Doubling as a flip book, stills of that animation filled a Rolodex located below the monitors. Section models and drawings covered the surface of the back-lit display. Located between each project were flat file drawers turned on their sides. When extracted from the case, these drawers revealed cross-sectioned perspective drawings. Located in the depths of the cases were DVD players, motors, mechanized models, and lights.

Geltner Loft

New York, New York

Old   New

The distinctiveness of this project was a creative response to budgetary constraints. LTL, working with the client, decided that only half of the loft should be renovated. Rather than attempting to seamlessly fuse new and old, this division—aligning with the overhang of the second-floor loft—established the territory of the renovation and produced a proscenium-like condition between the two sides of the apartment. This theatrical effect is intensified by the transformation of the existing ceiling of exposed joists into a luminous plane of translucent material backed by dimmable fluorescent lights that can be manipulated to selectively illuminate different areas of activity. Within this newly defined domestic stage, a series of linked elements are inserted: a steel-and-maple stair, a kitchen, and a wall of cabinetry for storage.

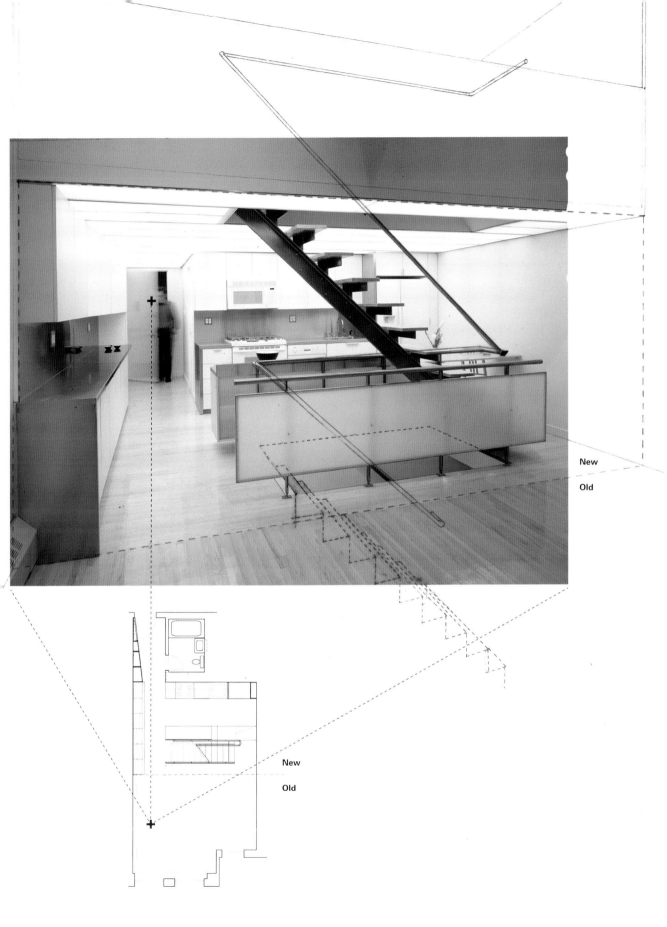

New

Old

New

Old

A single continuous steel railing links all three levels of the apartment. It doubles as a backsplash where it intersects with the stainless-steel kitchen counter. The stair is supported by a single steel stringer and detailed to minimize visual obstructions between the kitchen and dining area.

Old

New

The first and fourth treads of the new steel-and-maple stair extend out and produce the bottom and top of a cabinet that defines the outer edge of the kitchen. Paradoxically, climbing the stairs requires stepping on the surface plane of the kitchen counter.

The Great Egyptian Museum

Giza, Egypt

In 2003, 1,557 architecture firms from 83 countries entered this competition for a museum to house more than 120,000 Egyptian artifacts, including the treasures of King Tutankhamen, at a site adjacent to the Great Pyramids. The competition brief specified that the design for 4.3 million square feet of museum and landscape program must be presented on five A4 and five A5 pages, which works out to 3,000 square feet of program conveyed on each square inch of the submission. Given these representational constraints, the design had to be diagrammatically seductive and capable of being developed into a complex landscape and museum. It needed to be simultaneously obvious and intricate.

LTL's design for the museum is predicated on the spatial exchange between ground and sky. Both solid and hollow, occupiable pylons striate the site, while a canopy of solar glass collects and filters sunlight, and the dynamic interplay between these features creates a new museum landscape. The canopy of glass embedded with photovoltaics provides enclosure, filtered light, and a source of energy for this museum in the desert. A structural grid of inverted glass-clad wedges supports a space frame, creating an updated version of a hypostyle hall. Larger voids in the canopy bring exterior spaces to the interior of the museum, providing courtyards and moments of rest. Extended from stepped plateaus carved into the landscape, the stone-clad pylons link the landscape design with the museum proper. The pylons vary in height and width, creating a diverse set of spatial conditions appropriate for exhibition halls, archives, conference halls, and office areas.

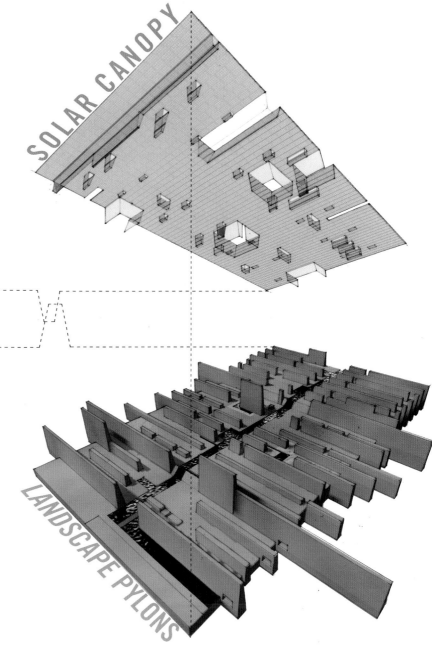

SOLAR CANOPY

LANDSCAPE PYLONS

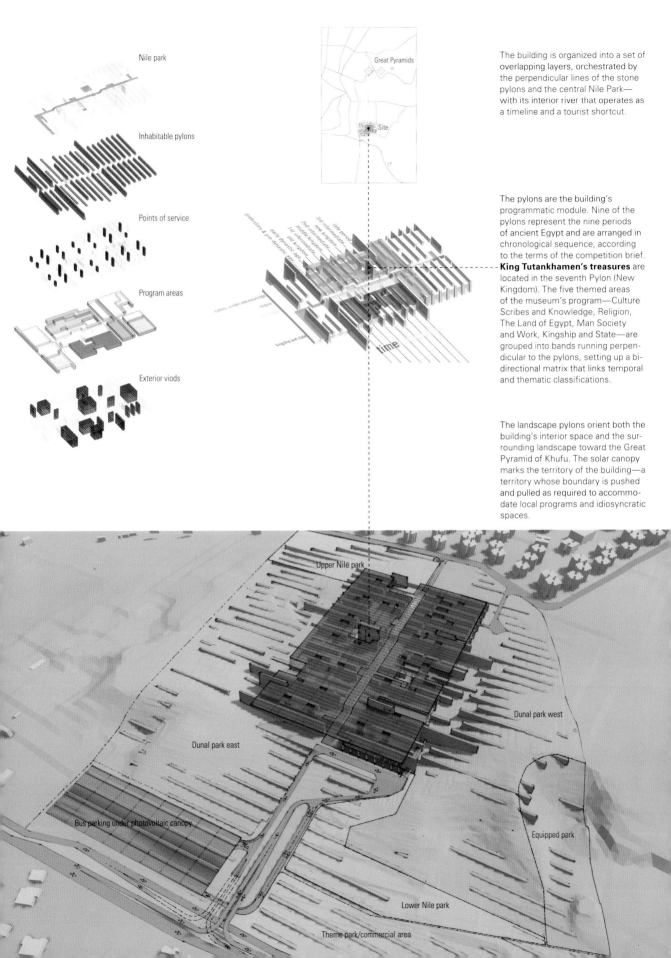

Nile park

Inhabitable pylons

Points of service

Program areas

Exterior viods

Great Pyramids

Site

prehistory & pre-dynastic age
1st kingdom
early dynastic
old kingdom
2nd intermediate
middle kingdom
3rd intermediate
new kingdom
late period

culture, scribes and knowledge

religion

kingship and state

time

The building is organized into a set of overlapping layers, orchestrated by the perpendicular lines of the stone pylons and the central Nile Park—with its interior river that operates as a timeline and a tourist shortcut.

The pylons are the building's programmatic module. Nine of the pylons represent the nine periods of ancient Egypt and are arranged in chronological sequence, according to the terms of the competition brief. **King Tutankhamen's treasures** are located in the seventh Pylon (New Kingdom). The five themed areas of the museum's program—Culture Scribes and Knowledge, Religion, The Land of Egypt, Man Society and Work, Kingship and State—are grouped into bands running perpendicular to the pylons, setting up a bi-directional matrix that links temporal and thematic classifications.

The landscape pylons orient both the building's interior space and the surrounding landscape toward the Great Pyramid of Khufu. The solar canopy marks the territory of the building—a territory whose boundary is pushed and pulled as required to accommodate local programs and idiosyncratic spaces.

Upper Nile park

Dunal park west

Dunal park east

Bus parking under photovoltaic canopy.

Equipped park

Lower Nile park

Theme park/commercial area

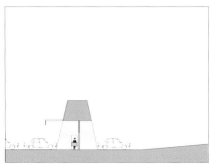

Sign and security gate

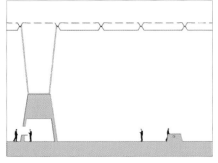

Museum entrance and offices

Coat check at entrance

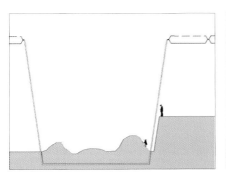

Dunal park in courtyard

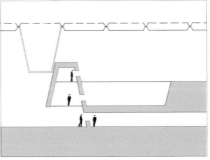

Exhibition display

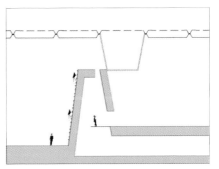

Pylon as climbing wall in park

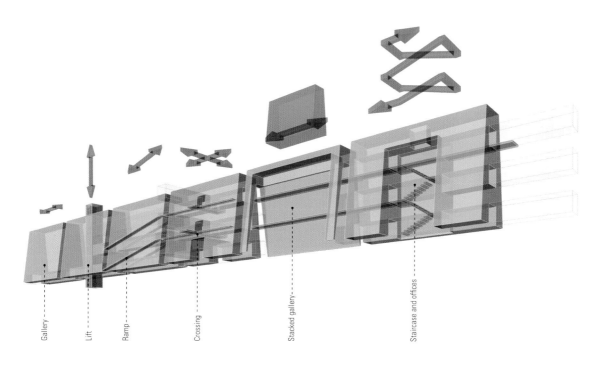

Gallery

Lift

Ramp

Crossing

Stacked gallery

Staircase and offices

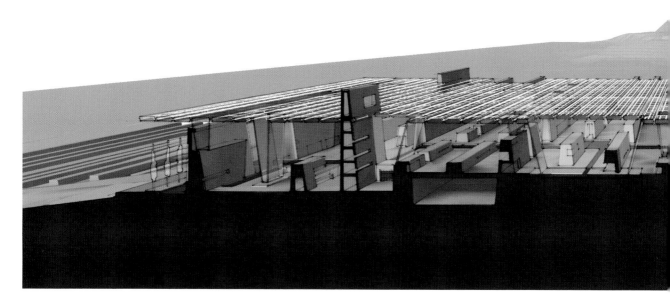

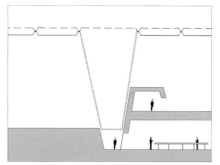

Conservation labs

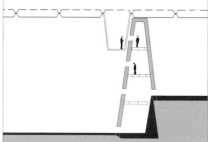

Nile crossing bridge

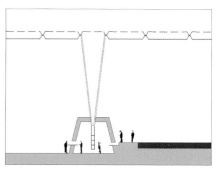

Gift shop

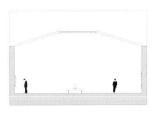

Traditional gallery

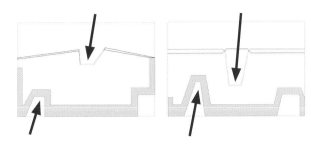

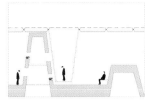

Great Egyptian gallery

The interaction of the stone pylons and the glass canopy provides an extensive repertoire of types of exhibition spaces and creates a wide variety of relationships between objects, observers, and landscapes. This is an implicit critique of the limitations of the hermetic rooms of traditional museums.

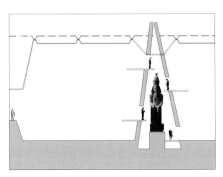

Exhibition display

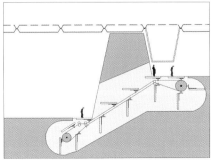

People movers

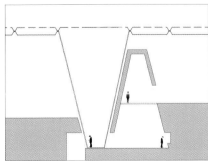

Exhibition display

The artifacts of King Tutankhamen's tomb are prominently displayed in the largest landscape pylon, which is located in the center of the building. A cafe and viewing platform at the top of the pylon align directionally with the three major pyramids of the Old Kingdom.

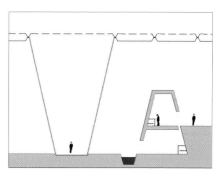

Exhibition display

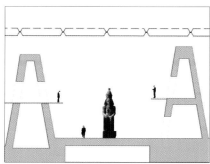

Exhibition display

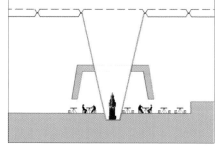

Cafe with exterior court

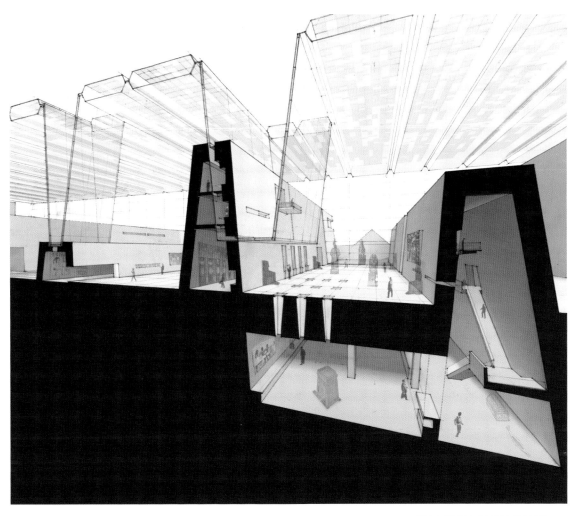

The exhibition spaces respond to the nature of the collection. The interior space of the pylon provides an intimate and enclosed space for funerary or domestic artifacts, while the broad expanses between the pylons provide ample space under the protective sun canopy for outdoor sculptures and large-scale works. The intersection of glass surfaces and the solid pylons creates vitrines for the display of smaller artifacts.

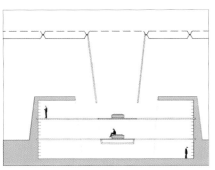

Library

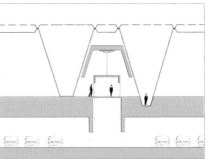

Elevator to underground garage

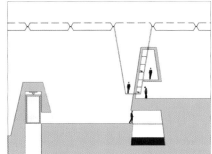

Exhibition display

Ini Ani
Coffee Shop

New York, New York

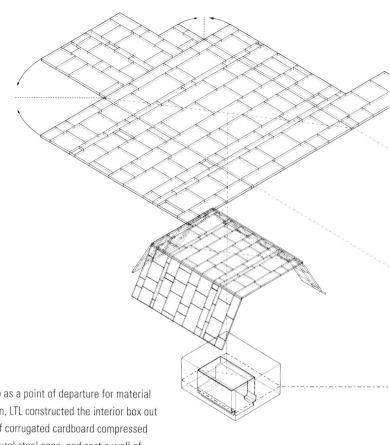

The design for this project was generated in response to the low budget, $40,000; site limitations, 350 square feet; and tight time frame, 3 months for design and construction. Furthermore, this pragmatic design process thoroughly intersected the fabrication process. When no suitable stock item was available within the client's budget, LTL designed and fabricated furniture to match the section of the built-in banquette and to make use of the same steel and wood employed in other aspects of the space.

Originally a fortune-teller's apartment and shop, the space was reconfigured by LTL as a room within a room, allowing both take-out traffic and a subdued lounge environment to coexist within the small footprint. Treating the disposable take-out coffee cup as a point of departure for material exploration, LTL constructed the interior box out of strips of corrugated cardboard compressed in a structural steel cage, and cast a wall of plaster coffee-cup lids as a sculptural feature at the entry.

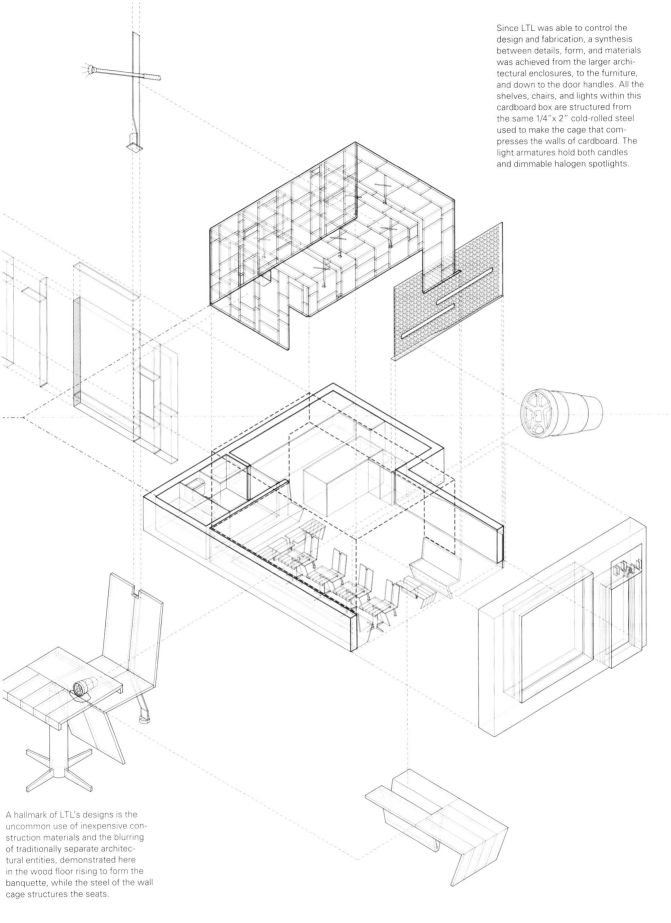

Since LTL was able to control the design and fabrication, a synthesis between details, form, and materials was achieved from the larger architectural enclosures, to the furniture, and down to the door handles. All the shelves, chairs, and lights within this cardboard box are structured from the same 1/4"x 2" cold-rolled steel used to make the cage that compresses the walls of cardboard. The light armatures hold both candles and dimmable halogen spotlights.

A hallmark of LTL's designs is the uncommon use of inexpensive construction materials and the blurring of traditionally separate architectural entities, demonstrated here in the wood floor rising to form the banquette, while the steel of the wall cage structures the seats.

The interior box of compressed cardboard and steel provides a lounge area nested within the larger space. An array of speakers is located above the box. The corrugations of the cardboard permit the sound to pass, while keeping the speakers hidden.

Steel parts were prefabricated off-site and assembled on site in two days using only countersunk screws. Over 25,000 strips of cardboard were pressed into the steel cage in one day, using the friction between the precise steel and the die-cut cardboard to hold the infill materials in place.

To the right as one enters, is a relief wall composed of 479 cast-plaster coffee cup lids. From a distance the wall appears to be a rhythmic sculptural panel, while up close it reveals a taxonomy of different solutions to the simple problem of keeping coffee in a cup. The unique diameter of each lid was individually drilled out of MDF sheets and was then skim coated to achieve the effect of a monolithic plaster wall. Attempts to cast the whole wall in solid tiles proved prohibitively heavy.

The architecture was detailed to tease out as many performative characteristics of banal common materials as possible. In addition to providing acoustic dampening, the corrugations of the cardboard strips allow the walls to appear transparent when viewed head on. Moreover, the repetition of thousands of pieces of cardboard provides a scale of detail and refinement that mitigates the relatively small size of the space.

Lozoo Restaurant

New York, New York

Located on the edge of SoHo in New York City, the existing space for this Shanghainese restaurant was a complex combination of six rooms with varying floor levels and ceiling heights spread over three properties. This assemblage of disparate rooms presented a potential problem for the unity of the restaurant; instead, this idiosyncratic quality of the space became the leitmotif of the design. In order to unify the separate spaces and to highlight the unique volumes of each room, LTL introduced a prominent horizontal line, a datum materialized as a 1/4-inch-thick stainless steel strip that cuts through the whole restaurant, providing a continuous visual reference.

The datum line sections the restaurant horizontally, with the lower half constructed from dark materials and the upper half in light materials. The white ceiling flows down and the dark floor rises up on each side to meet at the datum line, creating the sense of a space not determined by walls. Similarly, the datum engages and integrates the other significant components of the design: not only is it the joint between the floor material and the ceiling material, it also marks the top of the continuous felt banquette, the bar shelving, and the service station, as well as morphing into the collective sink.

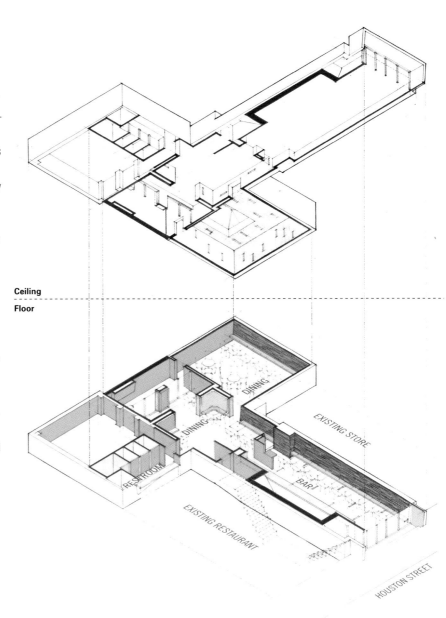

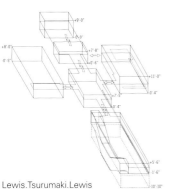

Above the datum line the high ceiling of the main dining room is wrapped in acoustical foam; linear incandescent lights set into the foam reveal its thickness.

Below, a 100'-long banquette is made from 10,000 linear feet of 3/4" felt strips. Translucent acrylic strips interspersed in these layers of the felt glow from lights located behind the banquette.

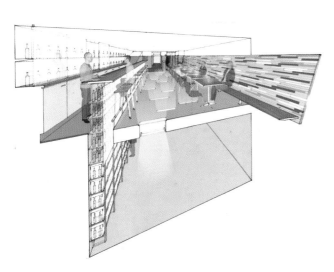

Because the height of the space that contains the bar made it difficult to place lights in the low ceiling, all the light comes from the floor, the banquette, the shelving, and the bar itself. Consequently, the ceiling is a smooth, unbroken surface. Acid-etched glass planks inlaid in the wood floor enable the work lights from the basement below to illuminate the bar.

The walnut bar is the top of a storage shelving unit, resting on the basement floor. An 8″ gap between the bar floor and the storage unit permits glimpses of the space below. Custom walnut-and-steel bar stools, designed and fabricated by LTL, are welded to linear glides. Augmented by rollerblade wheels, the stools slide back and forth along the foot-rail located above the gap.

Ceiling

Floor

In the back dining room an acrylic sculpture designed and built by LTL releases water at the datum line. The water runs down the surface of a 4"-thick block of sanded acrylic composed of 120 horizontal layers. Flowers lodged in voids cut into the acrylic block are kept fresh by the recirculating water.

A continuous sink made from folded stainless steel serves the toilets for both genders. The mirrors are mated with upside-down faucets. When they are turned on, water pours from the datum line down the mirror's reflective surface, blurring one's reflection and intensifying the visual pleasure experienced in the restaurant.

MSK Lobby Wall

New York, New York

LTL's installation for a feature wall in the lobby of the new Memorial Sloan-Kettering Cancer Center designed by Skidmore, Owings & Merrill responds to the specific opportunities and expectations of the new entrance space. The wall needed to be seductive while respecting the surrounding architectural materials and design. LTL's design takes advantage of the fact that the wall, dominating the views in the lobby, is visible from all sides. Vision itself is the generator for the design. 275 points were mapped through the plan of the lobby to reflect the density of circulation patterns. Each point in plan was then given a distinct elevation, with the overall set of raised points throughout the lobby mirroring the bell curve of human eye heights. These viewing moments were then connected

to an equal number of points mapped in an even grid across the front face of the feature wall. The connection between the viewing points and the feature wall was then considered as a view cone, whose cross-sectional diameter at its intersection with the wall is 5". The results of this operation are registered on and through the lobby wall. While the front surface shows the slight distortion of cones based on the angle of intersection in a highly structured grid, the rear surface shows the complex interpenetrations and overlaps between the 275 cones as they pass through the thickness of the wall. Complex digital engineering is necessary to fabricate the 480 unique steel boxes that comprise the 3'6"-deep, 30'-wide, 12'6"-tall sculptural wall.

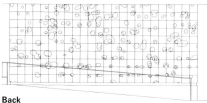

Back

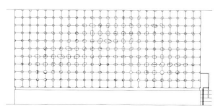

Front

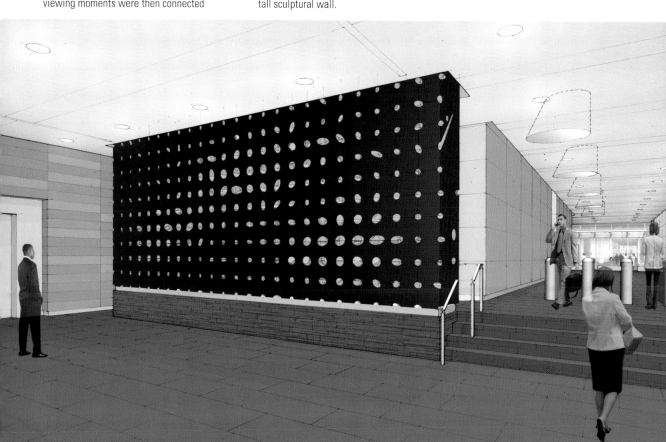

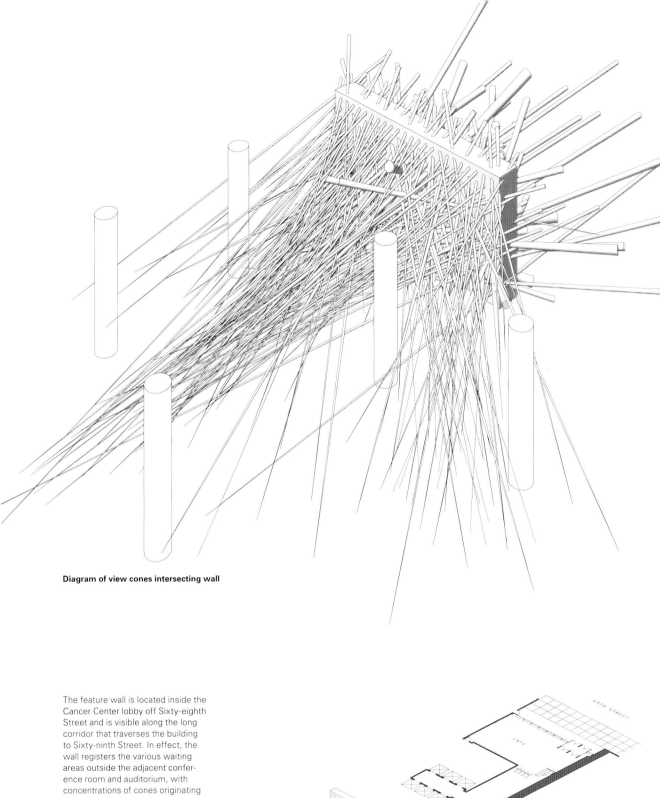

Diagram of view cones intersecting wall

The feature wall is located inside the Cancer Center lobby off Sixty-eighth Street and is visible along the long corridor that traverses the building to Sixty-ninth Street. In effect, the wall registers the various waiting areas outside the adjacent conference room and auditorium, with concentrations of cones originating at programmatically intense areas.

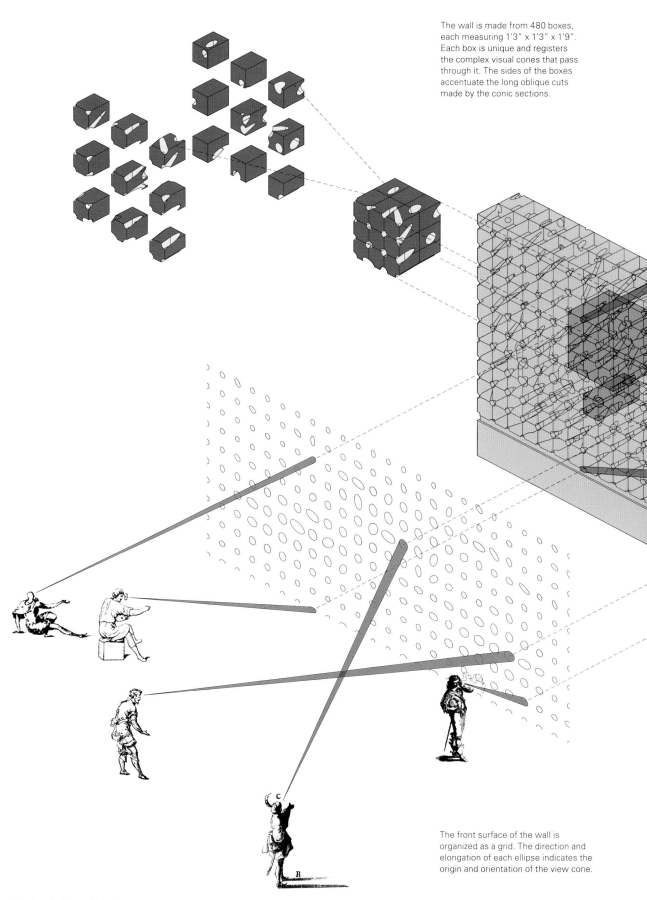

The wall is made from 480 boxes, each measuring 1'3" x 1'3" x 1'9". Each box is unique and registers the complex visual cones that pass through it. The sides of the boxes accentuate the long oblique cuts made by the conic sections.

The front surface of the wall is organized as a grid. The direction and elongation of each ellipse indicates the origin and orientation of the view cone.

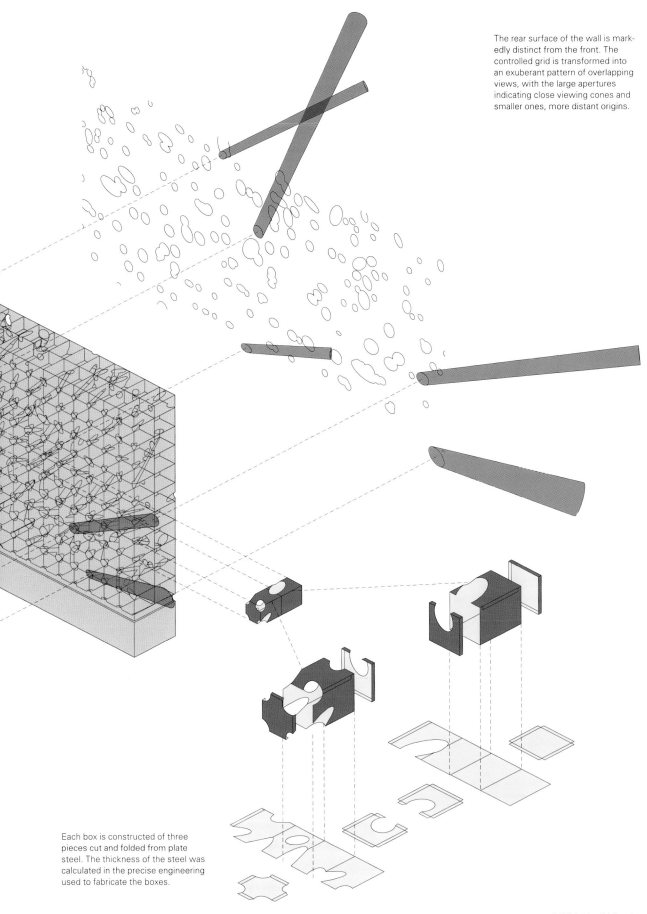

The rear surface of the wall is markedly distinct from the front. The controlled grid is transformed into an exuberant pattern of overlapping views, with the large apertures indicating close viewing cones and smaller ones, more distant origins.

Each box is constructed of three pieces cut and folded from plate steel. The thickness of the steel was calculated in the precise engineering used to fabricate the boxes.

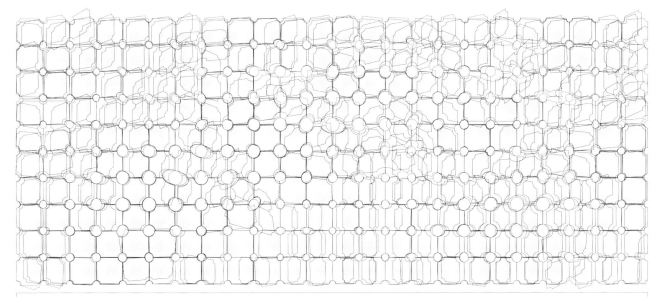

Composite elevation derived from 275 local perspectives

This drawing inverts the distortion inherent in the project. Drawn as if each of the 275 different perspective view cones were their own individual vanishing point, the intersection is a pure circle, while the distortion is registered here on the faces of the box, drawn as transparent overlapping planes.

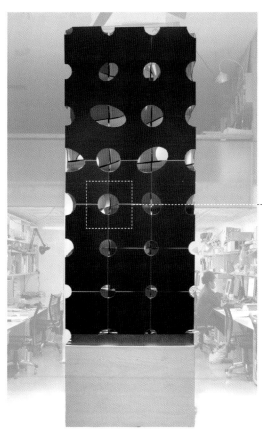

Back side of partial mock-up

Front side of partial mock-up

Interior view of mock-up

Each box is made from a front cap cut from 14-gauge stainless steel with black interference coating on a bead-blasted finish and a 4-sided body and interior cap cut from 14-gauge Azco "S" steel. The pieces are connected with exposed stainless steel fasteners that respond precisely to any conical intersections. The interior of the box is colored to maximize the legibility of the cuts and to illuminate the interior of the wall.

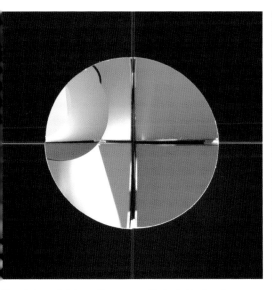

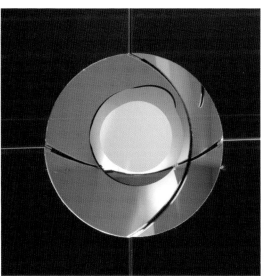

View into conic intersection, perpendicular to front surface

Seen perpendicular to the front, the viewing cone cuts obliquely to the front face, exposing the intersections of the sides of the boxes. The exit of this viewing cone at the back face is seen partially at the upper left.

The same intersection seen from along the line of the view cone

As one moves around the wall, angles of view match different view cones. At these moments, the elliptical cut on the front face of the wall is seen as a circle, matched by a receding circular tunnel cutting through the different boxes that make up the wall.

Nazareth House

Nazareth, Pennsylvania

This design for a 3,500-square-foot house for a retired couple in a typical developer subdivision is determined by two contradictory forces: the conventions of the suburban home and the peculiarities of its steeply sloping site. Rather than taking the more standard frontal position along the street, the house is rotated ninety degrees from the public edge and aligned with the topography, optimizing solar orientation and desirable views. The house is partially embedded in the landscape to form a protected rear terrace and to maximize southern exposure. Situated between two parallel retaining walls of local stone, the house is designed to produce either a condition of myopia or hyperopia; from within, it is only possible to see close up (into the terrace) or far away (the distant view). LTL intentionally sought to eliminate the middle ground of its immediate suburban context.

The portion of the house most directly visible from the public street is a garage door under a pitched roof—the icon of the suburban home and a facade design acceptable within the subdivision's by-laws. The shape and spatial qualities of the house change as one moves away from the street: from introverted to extroverted, from volume to surface, from compartmentalized private rooms to free-plan space, from pitched to inverted butterfly roof. Playing off the distinction between formal front and informal back typical of American homes, the design reconfigures and distorts familiar tropes of suburban domesticity and landscape.

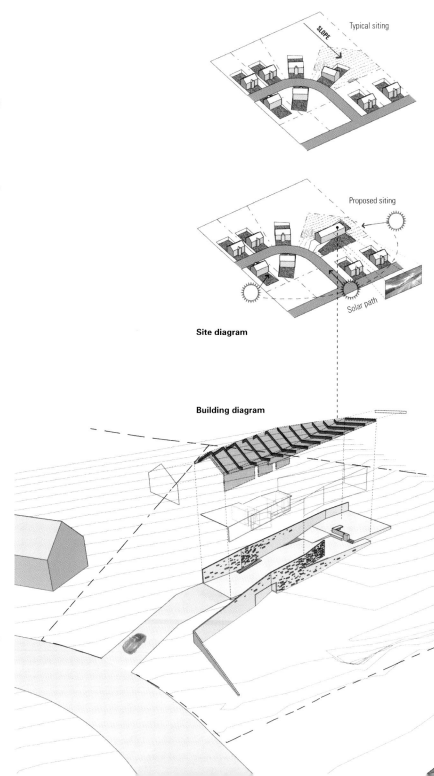

Typical siting

Proposed siting

Solar path

Site diagram

Building diagram

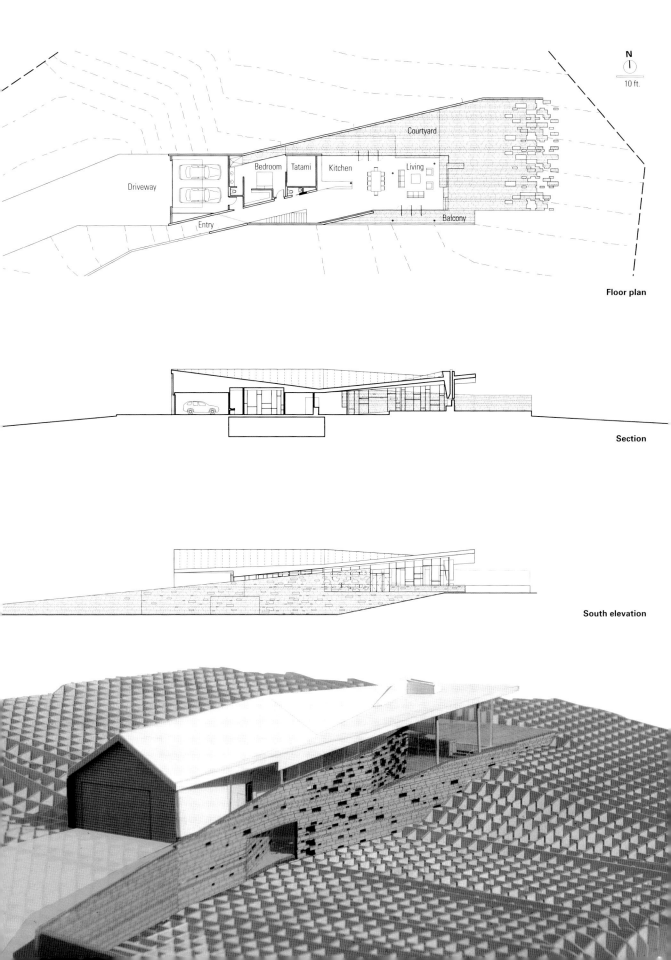

N
10 ft.

Floor plan

Driveway

Entry

Bedroom | Tatami | Kitchen

Courtyard

Living

Balcony

Section

South elevation

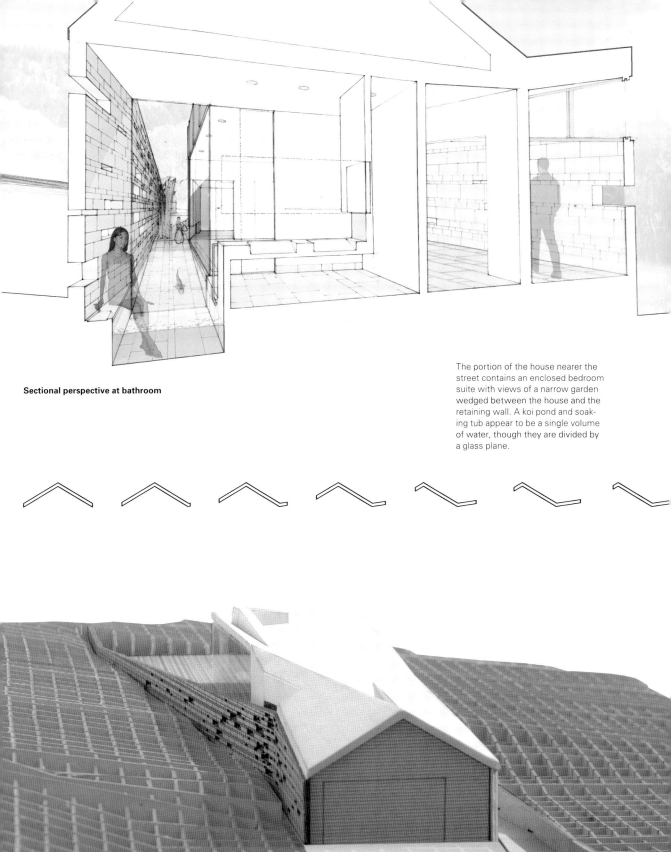

Sectional perspective at bathroom

The portion of the house nearer the street contains an enclosed bedroom suite with views of a narrow garden wedged between the house and the retaining wall. A koi pond and soaking tub appear to be a single volume of water, though they are divided by a glass plane.

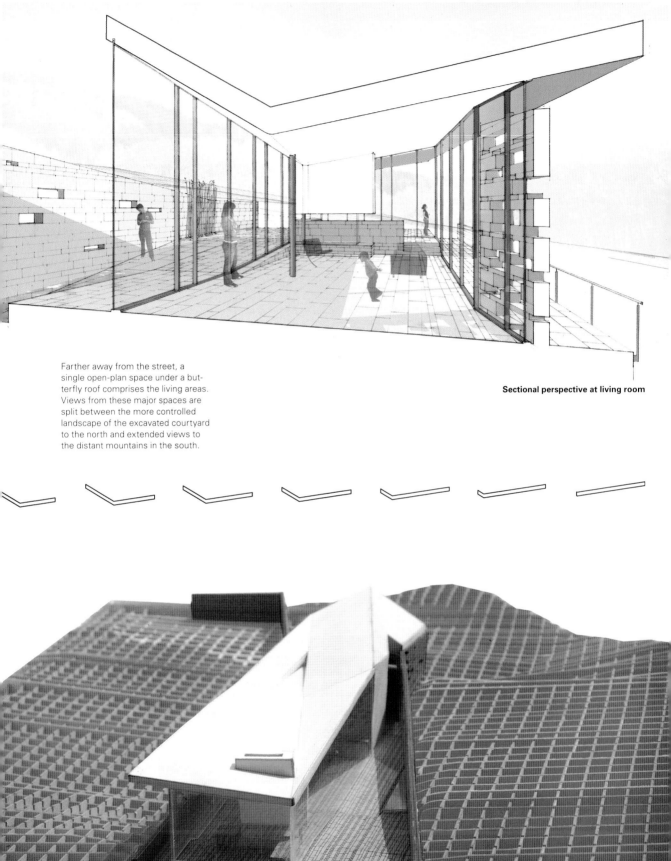

Farther away from the street, a single open-plan space under a butterfly roof comprises the living areas. Views from these major spaces are split between the more controlled landscape of the excavated courtyard to the north and extended views to the distant mountains in the south.

Sectional perspective at living room

The enclosing walls of the house change along their length as they respond to performative requirements; the wall serves as a retaining wall, an enclosure, and a screen. Akin to the exploits of the Three Little Pigs, material options were explored in order to test the structural and surface qualities latent within three different tectonic assembly systems.

Wood wall

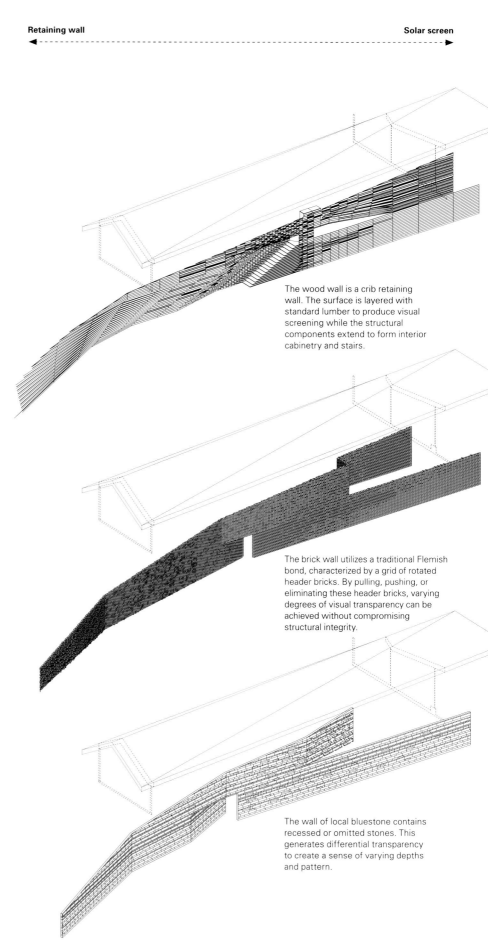

The wood wall is a crib retaining wall. The surface is layered with standard lumber to produce visual screening while the structural components extend to form interior cabinetry and stairs.

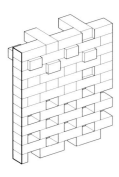

Brick wall

The brick wall utilizes a traditional Flemish bond, characterized by a grid of rotated header bricks. By pulling, pushing, or eliminating these header bricks, varying degrees of visual transparency can be achieved without compromising structural integrity.

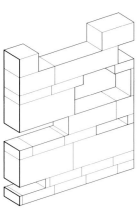

Stone wall

The wall of local bluestone contains recessed or omitted stones. This generates differential transparency to create a sense of varying depths and pattern.

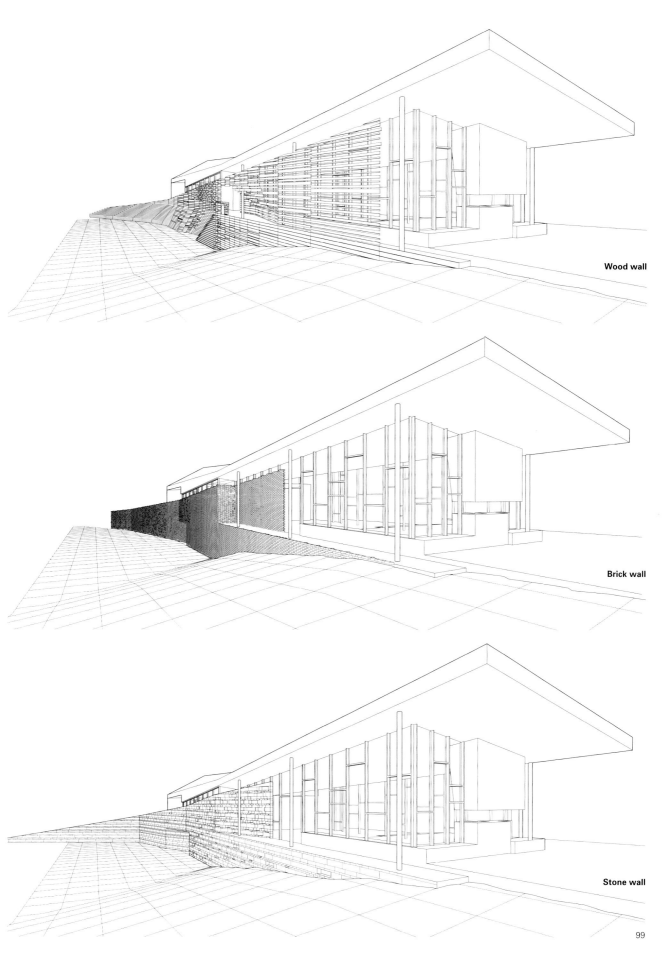

Wood wall

Brick wall

Stone wall

New Suburbanism

Prototypical American Suburb

What if the popular desires fueling the contemporary suburban culture of mini-mansions and big-box stores were creatively reconfigured? If the mega-store exists to service and supply the expanding landscape of mini-mansions, then why not combine the two, producing new efficiencies of land use, shared infrastructure, and reduced transportation without fighting the desires that feed the popularity of the quotidian suburb? Could the introduction of section to suburbia sponsor new vertical matings, creatively mitigating the excessive horizontal surfaces of suburban sprawl?

In this speculative proposal, dwellings migrate to occupy the vast horizontal roofscapes of the big boxes. The multifunctional aspect of the big-box construction system—once used only for warehouses and factories, but now adapted to build public libraries, schools, community centers, and gas stations—combined with the vast demand for housing means that the potential for the New Suburbanist coupling is enormous. The repetitive system of the big-box store's open-span structure with aisles and storage racks establishes a linear alignment of houses above. Storage structures extrude through the inhabitable roof plane of the big box, delineating property divisions within the

alternating pattern of houses and yards above and providing a container for the equipment and commodities of domestic life. In this hybrid of the logic of house and store, the identities of both are maintained, but in an altered form—now cross-wired to produce unanticipated social and spatial relationships through their mutual influence. In New Suburbanism, the logic of suburbia is exploited, wasteful redundancies are resolved, and new sectional matings are established in continued pursuit of the American Dream.

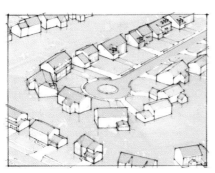

Mini-mansions ✛ Big-box stores

In New Suburbanism, individual houses reaccommodate existing desires, creatively reworking the normative suburban spatial logic determined by a culture of conspicuous consumption. Developer houses are conceived as an accumulation of figural commodity rooms and open public areas. The commodity rooms—formal living and dining rooms, master bedroom suites, media rooms, bathrooms—are treated like discrete consumer objects, independent and typically isolated within the house plan.

Commodity rooms ✛ Free-plan hangover

The more continuous public spaces—kitchen, foyer, breakfast rooms, and family rooms—are loosely treated as free plan, a hangover of a modern spatial sensibility. In the New Suburbanism proposal, the house arrangements are made through exploiting the reciprocal relationship between the figural commodity rooms and the free space of the public programs, initiating a spatial play not achieved in the stilted plans of typical homes. Thus, the object rooms reclaim a spatial imperative, without relinquishing their commodity or figural qualities.

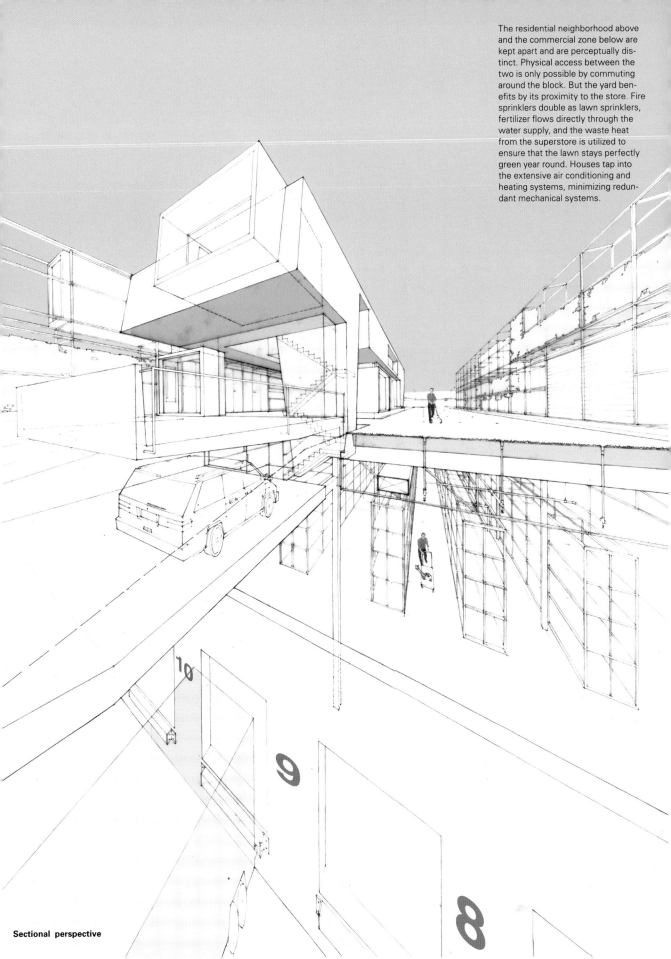

The residential neighborhood above and the commercial zone below are kept apart and are perceptually distinct. Physical access between the two is only possible by commuting around the block. But the yard benefits by its proximity to the store. Fire sprinklers double as lawn sprinklers, fertilizer flows directly through the water supply, and the waste heat from the superstore is utilized to ensure that the lawn stays perfectly green year round. Houses tap into the extensive air conditioning and heating systems, minimizing redundant mechanical systems.

Sectional perspective

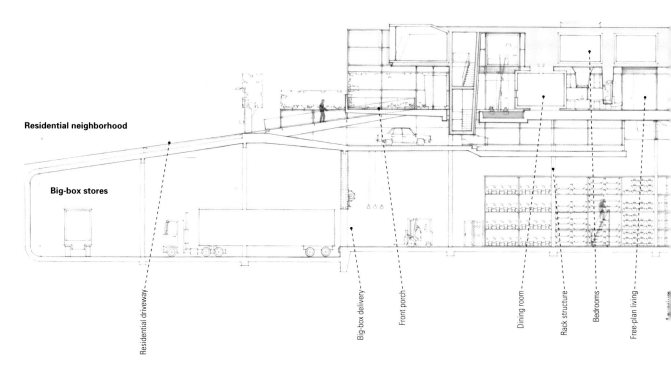

Residential neighborhood

Big-box stores

Residential driveway

Big-box delivery

Front porch

Dining room

Rack structure

Bedrooms

Free-plan living

In one speculative version of the house, on the ground level, the free-plan public spaces—living room, kitchen, foyer—are defined by the very location of the commodity rooms and objects—dining room, grand staircase, media cabinet, and fireplace. As figural, enclosed volumes, the commodity rooms' position in plan articulates the free-plan space. Owners can specify the exact types and number of commodity rooms that meet their needs, thereby also producing the idiosyncratic spatial quality of the entire house. This neighborhood plan shows three different ground-floor plans and one second-floor plan based simply on the quantity and location of the figural rooms. Furthermore, the interiors of each commodity room can be decorated in any manner desired—Louis XIV, *Wallpaper** moderne, or Martha Stewart Anglo-chic—independent from an overall decorating scheme, and separate from the decorating desires played out in the free-plan areas. This dialectic relationship allows for multiple versions of the New Suburban house within the given structural system, setting the stage for unprecedented mass customization.

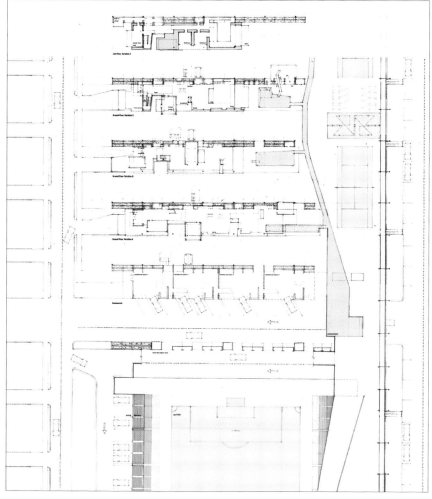

Residential plan

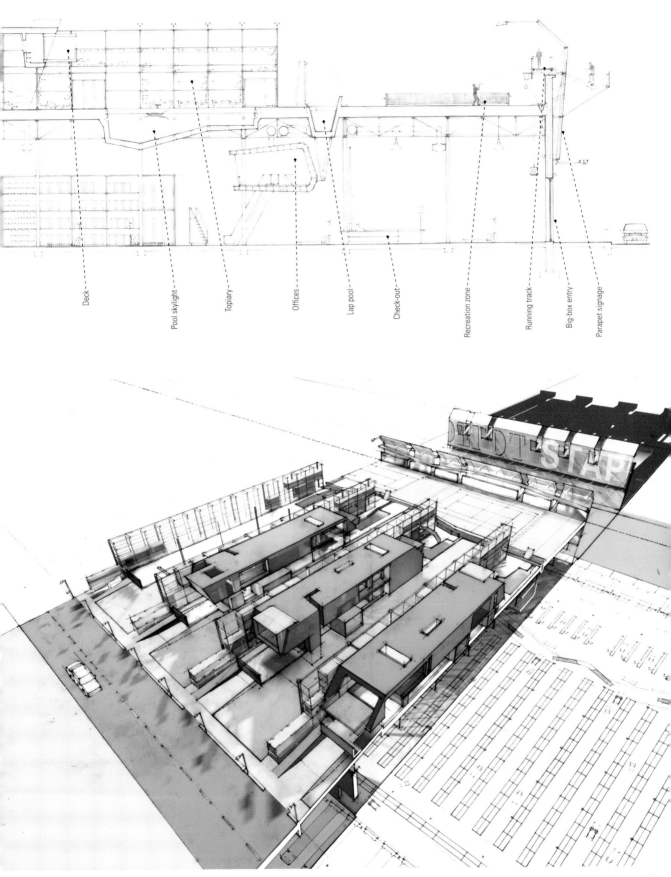

Deck

Pool skylight

Topiary

Offices

Lap pool

Check-out

Recreation zone

Running track

Big-box entry

Parapet signage

Sectional perspective

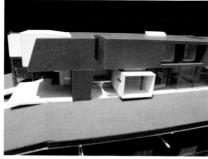

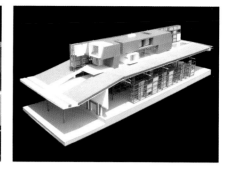

The massive and over-articulated roof is the icon of suburban mini-mansions, allowing double-height cathedral spaces and additional storage, while giving an umbrella of visual coherence after the fact to the commodity rooms assembled below.

The dominant roof mass is conceived from the start as a solid insulating zone, hung from the structural column grid and cocooning the private bedrooms and suites on the second floor. Volumes punch through the roof mass to produce the requisite double-height spaces for grand foyers and living rooms, while stalactite-like forms drop from the underside to accommodate storage, fireplaces and staircases on the first floor.

The linear organizing system of the big box reorients the conventional relationship between house and yard. The typically minimized zone of the side yard is here expanded to become the primary exterior space. The conventional distinction between the ornamental front yard and the private rear yard is eliminated in favor of a continuous functional space paralleling the long side of the house.

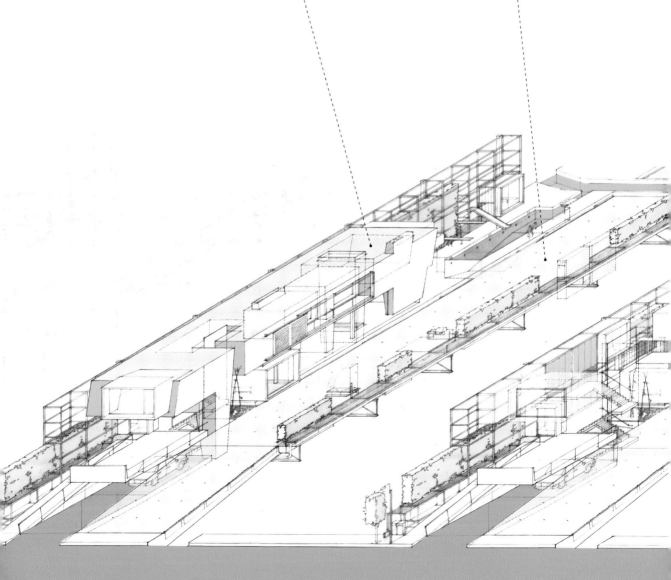

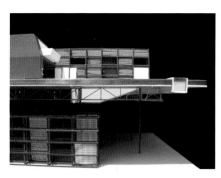

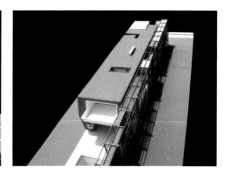

Private pools for each house are connected to a continuous lap pool, allowing a home owner on a sunny day to swim around the block. The pools double as skylights for the commercial space below.

Within the rooms of the typical sub-urban house, appliances, equipment, and objects determine occupation. Here the modular big-box storage racks are modified to become infra-structural walls containing all the necessary equipment for domestic life—appliances, cabinetry, fix-tures—as well as serving as points of connection to local utilities.

The racks provide a training ground for hedges and trees, establishing property divisions and avoiding potential turf wars over territory waged through lawn-care protocols. The racks are thus double sided, serving on one side the needs of the house, and on the other housing the necessary accessories of the neighboring suburban lawn: barbe-cue grills, hose bibs, garden sheds, and playground equipment.

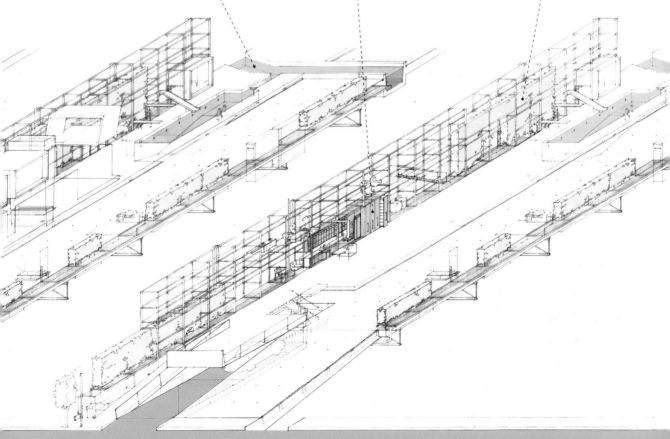

Sequential oblique projection

In the dialogue between free space and object rooms, the boundary distinguishing house and yard fluctuates, producing additional exchanges between interior and exterior. Analogous to the various decks, porches, and breezeways of the conventional house, these spaces bring the outside into the house as contained and encapsulated fragments of nature.

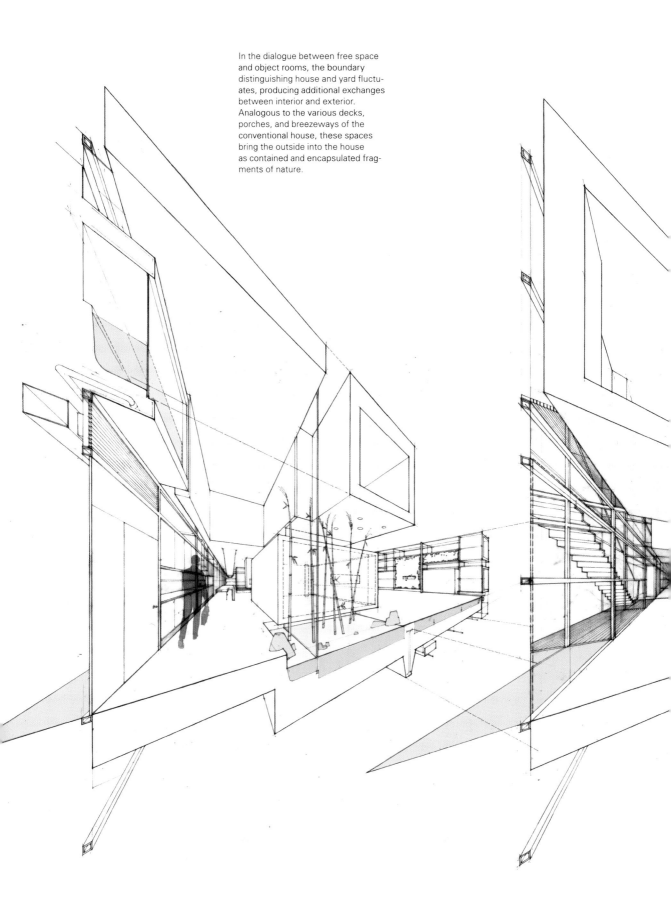

A void pushed down through the roof creates a pool—an internalized exterior aquarium—consistently filled with rainwater, and thus ideal for supporting small aquatic life.

The lawn takes full advantage of the deep plan of the big-box store below. The excess lawn extending beyond the racks, directly over the check-out counters of the stores, is the ideal zone for typical suburban recreations like tennis, shuffleboard, volleyball, and other community-oriented sports.

Sequential sectional perspectives

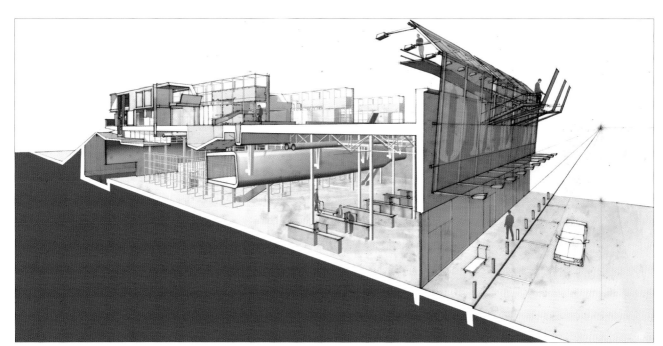

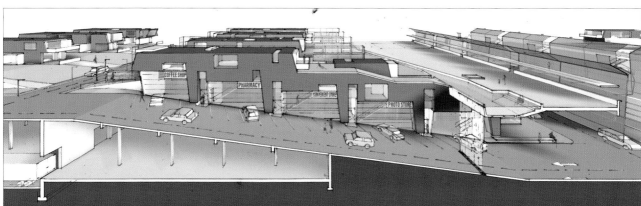

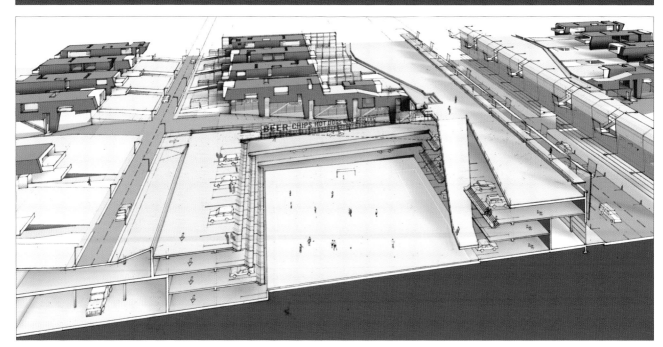

Sequential sectional perspectives

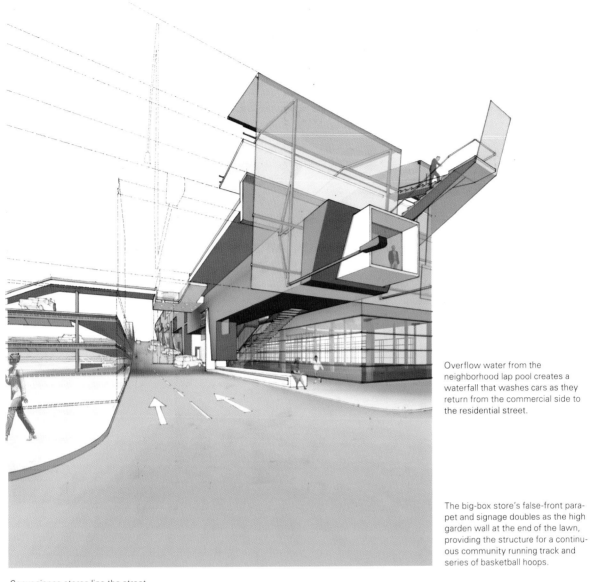

Overflow water from the neighborhood lap pool creates a waterfall that washes cars as they return from the commercial side to the residential street.

The big-box store's false-front parapet and signage doubles as the high garden wall at the end of the lawn, providing the structure for a continuous community running track and series of basketball hoops.

Convenience stores line the street that links the big-box commercial street below with the residential street above. The street also doubles as a ramp for the adjacent parking structure and sports field and provides quick access to goods and services on the short commute home.

The huge parking lots of big-box stores are reconfigured as a multistory parking structure around a central sports field, creating a new and more efficient hybrid of the suburban activities of shopping, sport spectatorship, and tailgate parties. In this stadium parking garage, parents can park and shop while their kids play within sight. The tailgate parties occur simultaneously in the bleachers of the sporting match and in the parking lot of the discount beer mart.

Wallcovering Collection for Knoll Textiles

LTL's collection of wallcovering designs for Knoll Textiles, entitled "Parallel Lines," explores the intersection between decoration and drawing. The collection is based on the prohibition against marking on walls, a prohibition wallcoverings are frequently employed to enforce. Each pattern is produced through the digital repetition of a select number of scanned hand-drafted graphite lines. The patterns exhibit manual flaws and digital precision and have a built-in spatial play and a resolution that allows different readings: up close the detail of variations of the pencil work and logic of the pattern is visible; from afar the pattern has subtle spatial and optical effects.

Margin reads as a series of vertical columns produced, paradoxically, by horizontal lines. The lines exhibit a drafting convention where the end and beginning of each is emphasized. This accentuates the verticality of the pattern.

Perimeter is based on nine rect-
angles, each with a different line
type and dimensions, overlapped
and layered to provide a sense of
depth. The line types are architectural standards, each possessing
a different meaning, from marking
a legal territory to an overhang to a
movement path.

Vector uses only seven different
pencil lines. Each represents an
attempt to draw a line by hand
that consistently faded from dark
to light. The seven lines were
scanned and digitally replicated
to produce the appearance of an
undulating field that moves up
and down the wall.

Parking Sections

U.S. Pavilion, Venice Biennale, Italy

For the 2004 Venice Architectural Biennale, *Architectural Record*, curator of the United States Pavilion, chose six firms and asked each to rethink a different building type. LTL was assigned the courtyard space and task of exploring the future of the parking garage. Although prominently positioned, the courtyard presented problems for the display of architectural representations, not the least of which were the lack of conventional exhibit walls, unpredictable weather, and the neoclassical features of the courtyard. Recognizing the necessity of using these challenges to generate the installation design, LTL decided to engage the neoclassical columns dominating the courtyard in order to subvert the building's architectural authority. Using the entasis and stability of the four entrance columns,

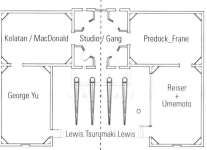

Kolatan / MacDonald   Studio/ Gang   Predock_Frane

George Yu

Reiser
+
Umemoto

Lewis.Tsurumaki.Lewis

LTL extended a twenty-foot-long cantilevered aluminum frame from each, wrapping both sides of each frame in exterior-grade vinyl printed with high-resolution images. The right side of each armature displays a project exploring the potential of parking in section, while the left side depicts a photographic analysis of the problems and pleasures of parking in plan. With these extensions, the Doric columns are split in half, their geometry elaborated, and their iconic presence hidden. The colonnade was thus transformed into corridors for both viewing and for accessing the building.

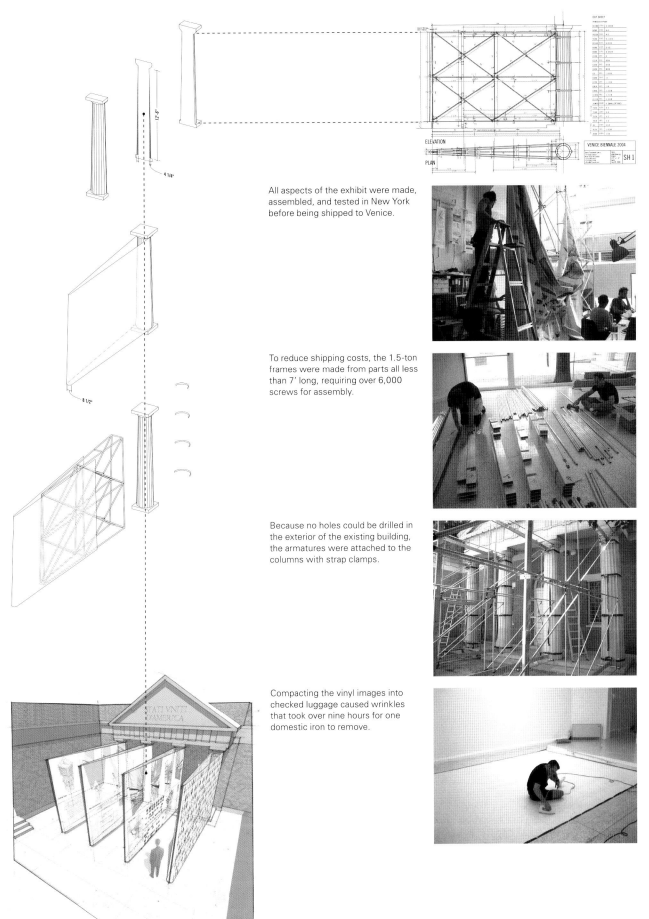

All aspects of the exhibit were made, assembled, and tested in New York before being shipped to Venice.

To reduce shipping costs, the 1.5-ton frames were made from parts all less than 7' long, requiring over 6,000 screws for assembly.

Because no holes could be drilled in the exterior of the existing building, the armatures were attached to the columns with strap clamps.

Compacting the vinyl images into checked luggage caused wrinkles that took over nine hours for one domestic iron to remove.

Zooming in by powers of ten, four panels of aerial photographs analyzed the physical and cultural problems and pleasures of parking when viewed in plan—from big box parking sprawl to field patterns of parking to crime and copulation in parking lots, to tailgate parties.

The slope of the column is continued in the slope of each image panel. At the end of each panel was located a 1/2"-thick vertical aluminum bar, thereby making it possible to measure the slope of the column based on the width of visible aluminum.

2,378 air fresheners, donated by the Car-Freshner Corporation, were aggregated into a mosaic depicting a section through a full-scale 1972 red Volkswagen Beetle. The car was imaged at the resolution of an air freshener pixel.

Three speculative projects explored the architectural and urban potentials of parking when designed primarily through an emphasis of the section: Tourbus Hotel, Park Tower, and New Suburbanism.

The narrow space between the panels, as well as their height, required that the images on the upper portions of the panels be anamorphically distorted in order to appear correct from below.

1 M² OF BIG-BOX RETAIL REQUIRES 1 M² PARKING. AT CURRENT GROWTH RATES, IKEA, WALMART, HOME DEPOT, TARGET AND KMART WILL COVER THE AREA OF SWITZERLAND IN 40 YEARS.

US DRIVERS SPEND 8+ BILLION HOURS PER YEAR STUCK IN TRAFFIC. 25% OF URBAN TRAFFIC CONGESTION IS CAUSED BY PEOPLE SEARCHING FOR PARKING.

80% OF CRIME AT SHOPPING MAELS AND OFFICE PARKS OCCURS IN THE PARKING LOT. A PARKED CAR IS THE SECOND MOST POPULAR SITE TO CONCEIVE A CHILD.

FOR 96 HOURS, OVER 100,000 PEOPLE TAILGATE IN THE PARKING LOT OF THE FLORIDA-GEORGIA FOOTBALL GAME. THE GAME RUNS ABOUT 3.5 HOURS WITH LESS THAN 75,000 FANS.

Park Tower

Prototypical American City

For the U.S. Pavilion at the 2004 Venice Architectural Biennale *Architectural Record* commissioned LTL to imagine the future of the parking garage. Using the possible future of clean and quiet hydrogen fuel as a catalyst, Park Tower envisions a drive-up skyscraper, intertwining a parking garage with a mixed-use sequence of programs, all without noxious fumes or excessive engine noise. Suburban patterns are thus coupled with an urban building type and footprint. The time-consuming suburban commute is transformed into a seductive urban ascent, complete with panoramic views.

The ubiquitous nature of automobiles has created a series of complex proportional relationships between the size and type of architectural programs and required parking sizes and numbers. While the dependency of program type and parking is statistically coupled and legislated into building and zoning codes, the potential reciprocal spatial relationship between parking and architectural program has been left under-exploited. What if the interdependence of spatial function and parking space becomes the catalyst for architectural invention? Instead of sequestering parking to subterranean levels, what if automobile parking is intertwined into every level of a building, changing in density and frequency to match the required parking allocations of divergent programs of a complex, multi-use Park Tower?

While employing a commonplace mix of programs—retail space on the ground level, hotel and office space in the middle, and residential on the top—the Tower intertwines in the manner of a double helix, a

drive-through parking garage and a sandwich of inhabitable space. The sectional matings of each program's function and parking are maximized based on the specific ratio of parking to program type. To facilitate rapid ascent and descent, an additional speed-lane wraps up through the tower, allowing the penthouse owner to drive home in the manner of a trip to the top of Hollywood Hills or the outdoor enthusiast to experience the roof-top testing ground.

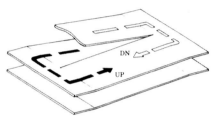

Parking garage diagram

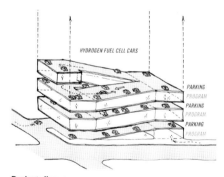

Project diagram

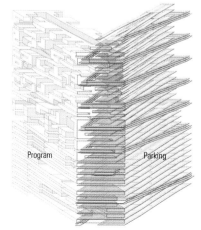

Spliced oblique projection

Residential

Office

Hotel

Retail

Building DNA

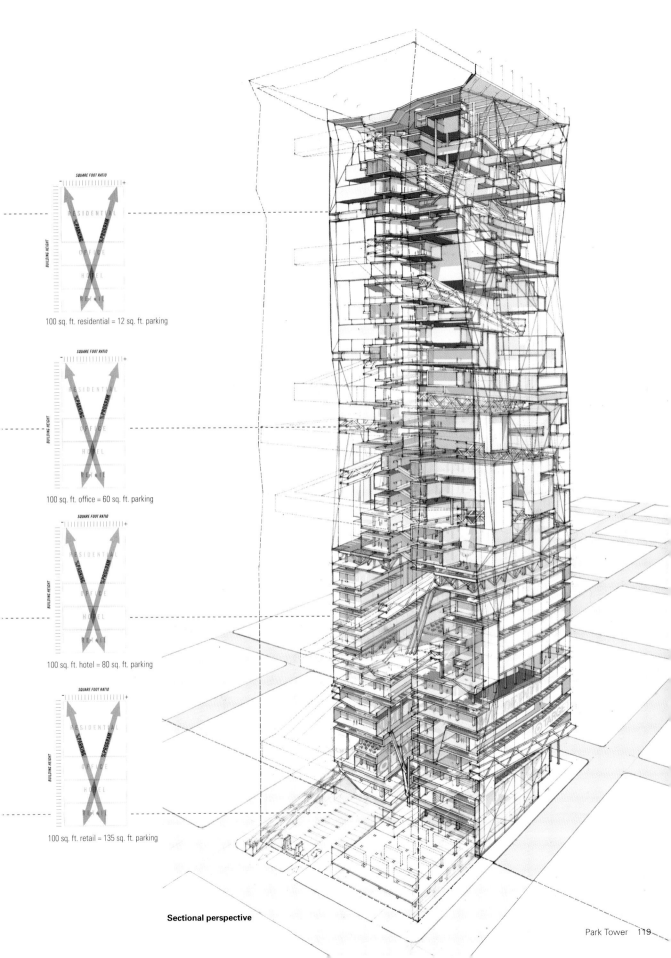

SQUARE FOOT RATIO

100 sq. ft. residential = 12 sq. ft. parking

SQUARE FOOT RATIO

100 sq. ft. office = 60 sq. ft. parking

SQUARE FOOT RATIO

100 sq. ft. hotel = 80 sq. ft. parking

SQUARE FOOT RATIO

100 sq. ft. retail = 135 sq. ft. parking

Sectional perspective

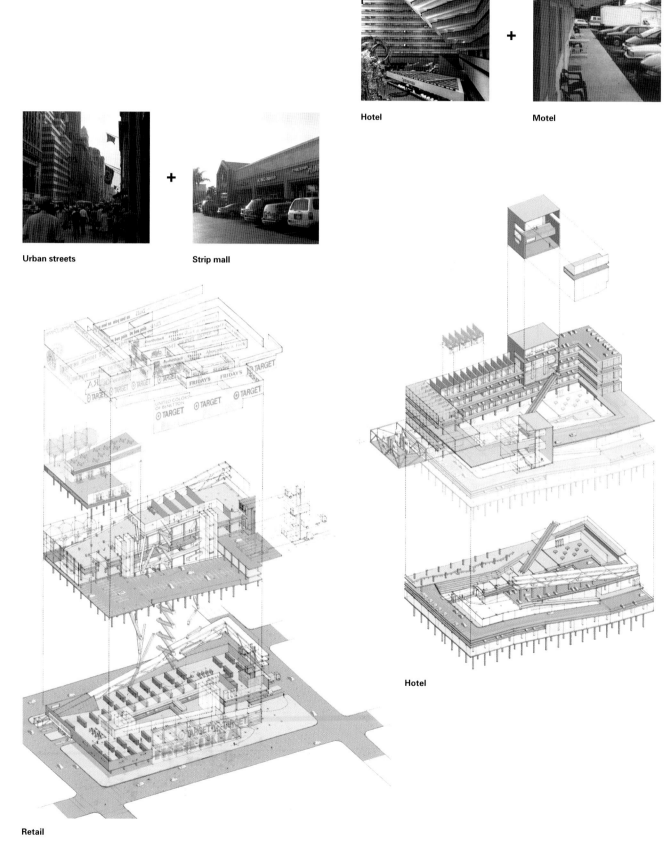

Hotel

Motel

Urban streets

Strip mall

Hotel

Retail

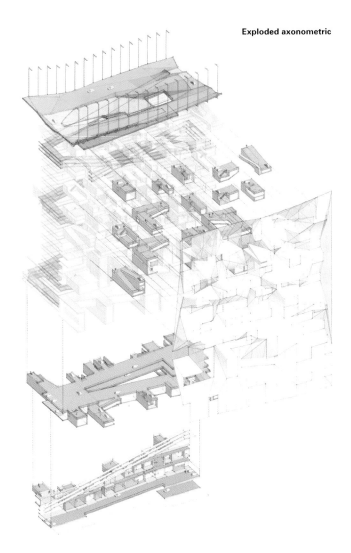

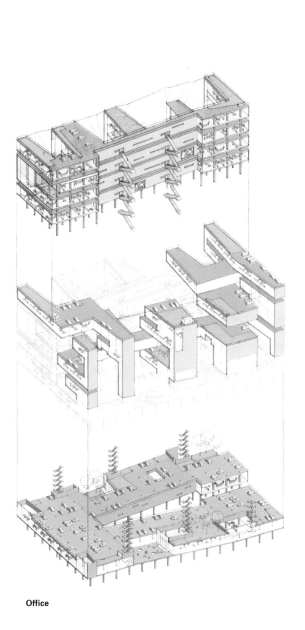

Office

Residential

High-rise living

Drive-in living

Office tower

Office park

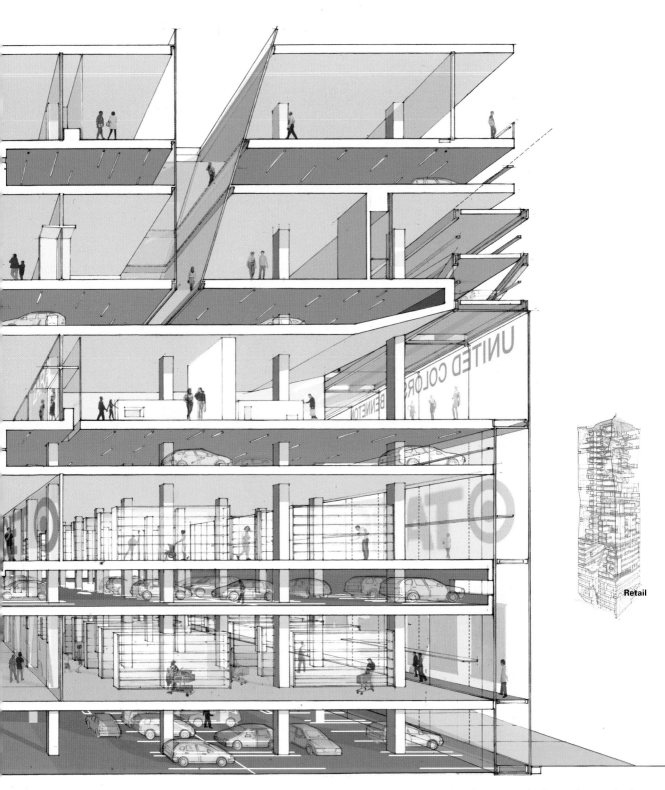

Retail

The retail district splices a strip mall with an urban shopping street. Due to the double helix, every parking space has close proximity to the stores. A series of escalators rotate through the central atrium, allowing shoppers to seamlessly move between levels. Exterior courtyards introduce green space into the retail spiral and produce complex interactions between the interior and exterior facades of stores.

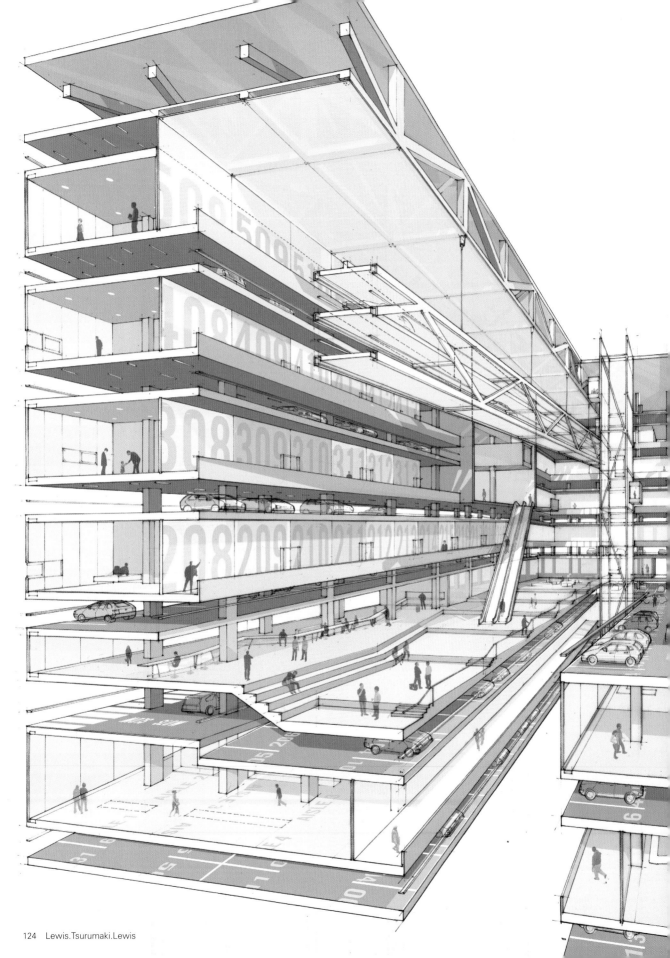

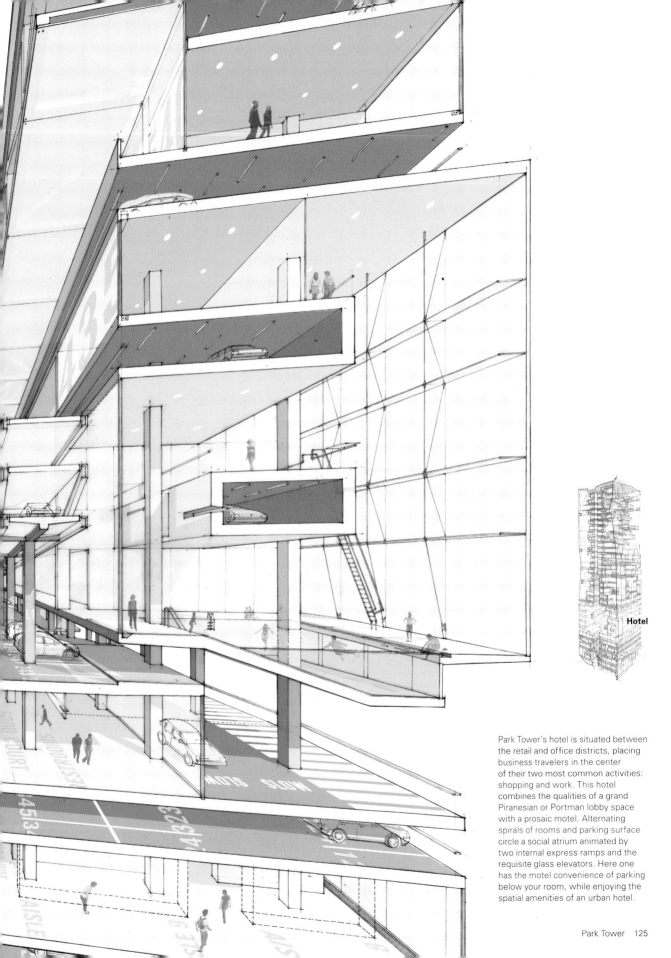

Hotel

Park Tower's hotel is situated between the retail and office districts, placing business travelers in the center of their two most common activities: shopping and work. This hotel combines the qualities of a grand Piranesian or Portman lobby space with a prosaic motel. Alternating spirals of rooms and parking surface circle a social atrium animated by two internal express ramps and the requisite glass elevators. Here one has the motel convenience of parking below your room, while enjoying the spatial amenities of an urban hotel.

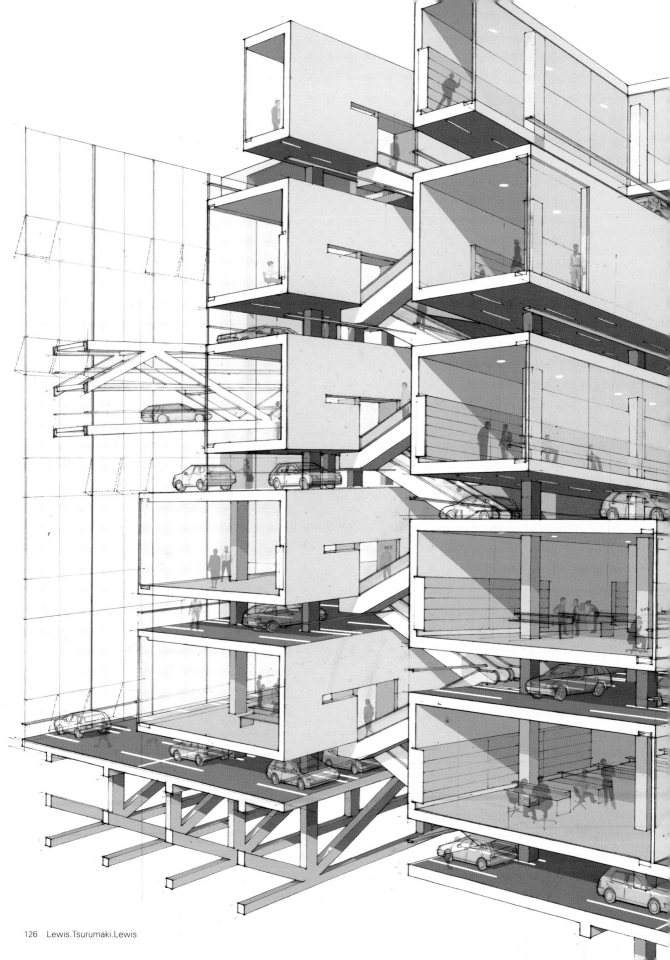

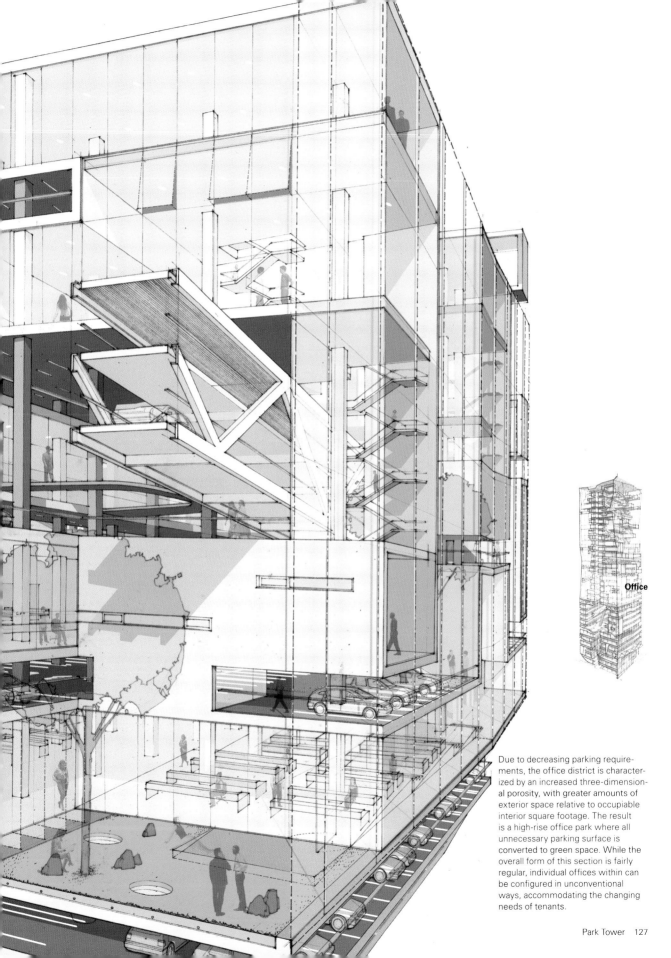

Office

Due to decreasing parking requirements, the office district is characterized by an increased three-dimension-
al porosity, with greater amounts of
exterior space relative to occupiable
interior square footage. The result
is a high-rise office park where all
unnecessary parking surface is
converted to green space. While the
overall form of this section is fairly
regular, individual offices within can
be configured in unconventional
ways, accommodating the changing
needs of tenants.

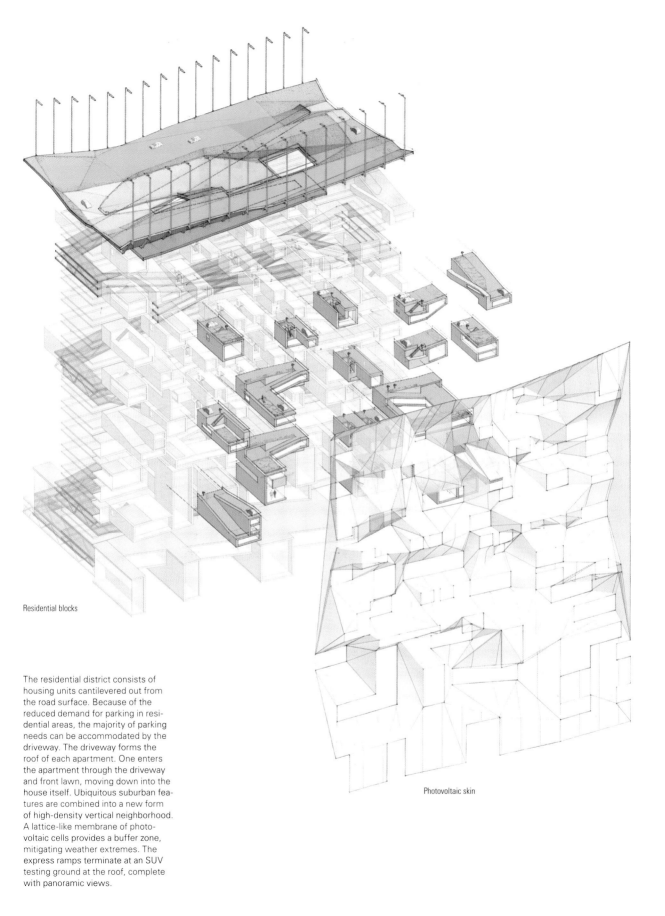

Residential blocks

Photovoltaic skin

The residential district consists of housing units cantilevered out from the road surface. Because of the reduced demand for parking in residential areas, the majority of parking needs can be accommodated by the driveway. The driveway forms the roof of each apartment. One enters the apartment through the driveway and front lawn, moving down into the house itself. Ubiquitous suburban features are combined into a new form of high-density vertical neighborhood. A lattice-like membrane of photovoltaic cells provides a buffer zone, mitigating weather extremes. The express ramps terminate at an SUV testing ground at the roof, complete with panoramic views.

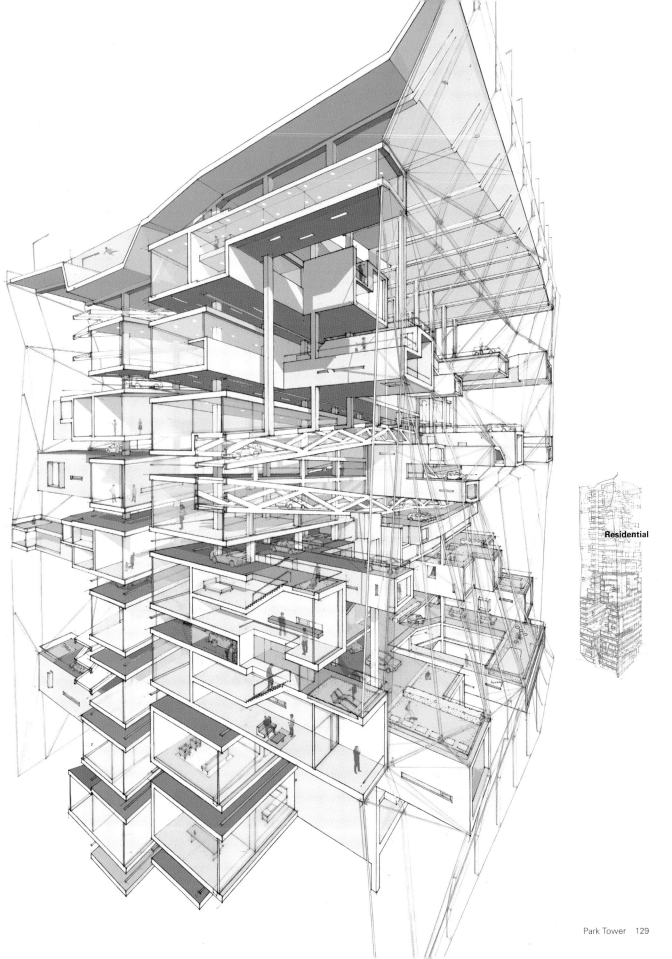

Residential

Tides Restaurant

New York, New York

Located in New York's Lower East Side, this project presented the unusual challenge of designing a 22-seat restaurant in a tiny 420-square-foot room where the ceiling is higher than the space is wide. In order to counter the potentially claustrophobic dimensions of this space, LTL decided to make the ceiling the dominant feature of the project. Playing off the name "Tides," the ceiling was designed to create a topographical effect that evokes an inverted field of sea grass. This effect was achieved by aggregating bamboo skewers in carefully calculated patterns to form a dense intricate ceiling seascape. Various other types of bamboo are used throughout the space; caramelized bamboo flooring folds up to become the booth seats and banquette backs, and a lighter shade of bamboo flooring covers the upper half of the banquette wall. Individual planks pull away from the wall, revealing lights. The bottom half of each table is translucent acrylic, which pipes the light of a candle encased in the bamboo plywood top to the edge of the table. The table magnifies the candle light, intensifying the most flattering form of restaurant lighting.

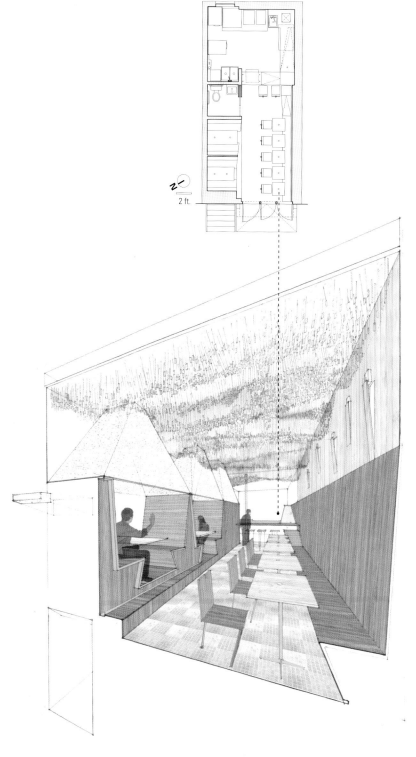

2 ft.

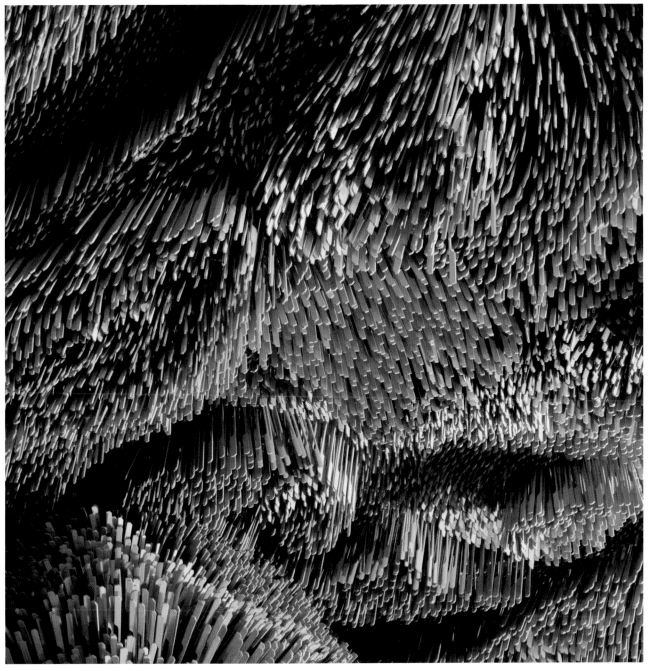

The ceiling topography required more than 110,000 bamboo skewers—identical to those used in the kitchen. Each skewer was individually dipped in glue and inserted into translucent 2″-thick ceiling panels, which were placed into a dropped ceiling frame.

Each skewer's placement was carefully calibrated according to depth, orientation, and tilt to produce a continuous pattern across the panels simulating tidal flows, eddies, and channels.

Acoustical material and skewers form three pyramidal volumes covering two booths and the bathroom, increasing the sense of intimacy and privacy within the restricted space. The steel structure inside the cones extends to form supports for dimmable linear lights.

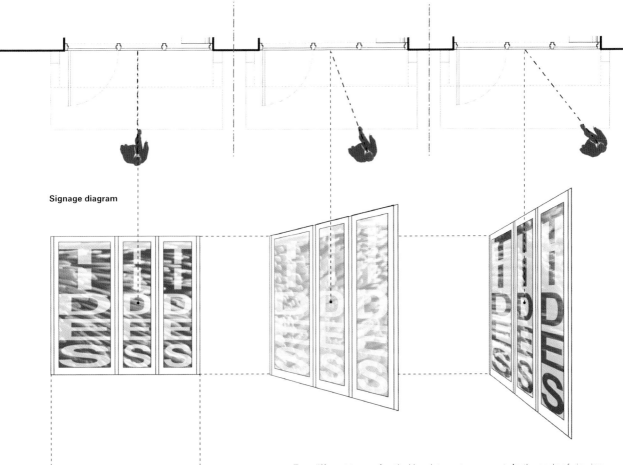

Signage diagram

Two different types of optical Lumisty film turn the restaurant's door and windows into a seductive yet subtle sign. Viewed straight on, the letters are opaque and their background is transparent. As the angle of viewing changes, so does the balance of opacity and transparency, until the reverse is true.

Tourbus Hotel

Between Munich and Venice

The standard bus tour of Western Europe condenses the diverse range of countries into a series of tourist sites suspended within a network of highways and hotels, souvenir shops, and service stops. The thousands of tour buses that traverse this space trace out the same routes again and again with only minor variations, packaging significant cities into eight-to eighteen-day circuits. These itineraries treat the continent the way a subway map describes a city: a space structured as points of interest separated by long interludes of memory and anticipation. An hour-by-hour analysis of one thirteen-day tour revealed that more time was actually spent on the bus than in cities. Moreover, most hotels were located on the periphery of the cities, making casual excursions into the city difficult and thereby rein-forcing the social heterotopia of the bus tourists.

Rather than lament or ignore these conditions, the Tourbus Hotel is a new building type designed to accommodate the logistics of the bus tour and the com-plex social and visual mechanisms of the tour bus. A speculative prototype, the Tourbus Hotel, located opportunistically on the highways between major tour-ist sites, plugs into the existing routes of European bus tours. The design and organization of the building is predicated on the fact that everyone in the hotel has come from, or is going to, the same two cities, for example between Venice and Munich. However different the tourists may be from each other, they all share

the same memory or anticipation of the same two cities. The building is composed of three zones—a bus parking level, a social lobby level, and a zone of hotel bars—each split equally to formalize the Janus nature of the program: coming and going, memory and anticipation, Venice and Munich.

Map of European bus tours

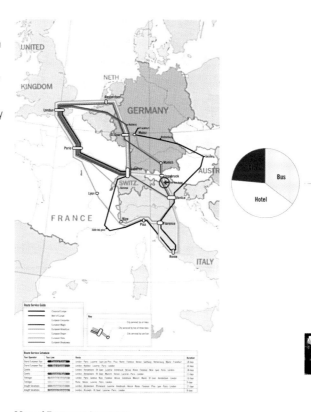

Analysis of eight-day Kontiki European bus tour, July 2003

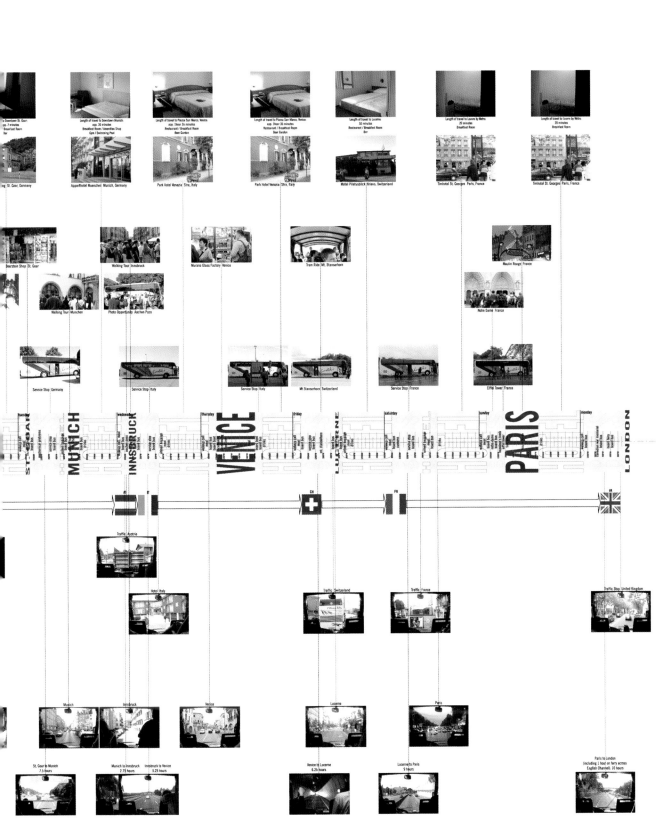

Length of travel to Downtown St. Goar:
app. 7 minutes
Breakfast Room
Bar

Length of travel to Downtown Munich
app. 30 minutes
Breakfast Room
Gym / Swimming Pool

Length of travel to Piazza San Marco, Venice
app. 1hour 30 minutes
Restaurant / Breakfast Room
Beer Garden

Length of travel to Piazza San Marco, Venice
app. 1hour 30 minutes
Restaurant / Breakfast Room
Beer Garden

Length of travel to Lucerne
30 minutes
Restaurant / Breakfast Room
Bar

Length of travel to Louvre by Metro
20 minutes
Breakfast Room

Length of travel to Louvre by Metro
20 minutes
Breakfast Room

ng. St. Goar, Germany

Apparthotel Muenchen Munich, Germany

Park Hotel Venezia Stra, Italy

Park Hotel Venezia Stra, Italy

Hotel Pilatusblick Kriens, Switzerland

Timhotel St. Georges Paris, France

Timhotel St. Georges Paris, France

Beerstein Shop St. Goar

Walking Tour Innsbruck

Murano Glass Factory Venice

Tram Ride Mt. Stanserhorn

Moulin Rouge France

Walking Tour Munchen

Photo Opportunity Aachen Pass

Notre Dame France

Service Stop Germany

Service Stop Italy

Service Stop Italy

Mt. Stanserhorn Switzerland

Service Stop France

Eiffel Tower France

tuesday   wednesday   thursday   friday   saturday   sunday   monday

ST. GOAR   MUNICH   INNSBRUCK   VENICE   LUCERNE   PARIS   LONDON

AT   IT   CH   FR   UK

Traffic Austria

Hotel Italy

Traffic Switzerland

Traffic France

Traffic Stop United Kingdom

Munich   Innsbruck   Venice   Lucerne   Paris

St. Goar to Munich
7.5 hours

Munich to Innsbruck
2.75 hours

Innsbruck to Venice
5.25 hours

Venice to Lucerne
6.25 hours

Lucerne to Paris
9 hours

Paris to London
(including 1 hour on ferry across
English Channel): 10 hours

Hotel bars and glass skin

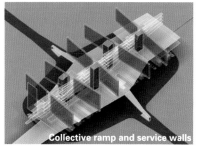

Collective ramp and service walls

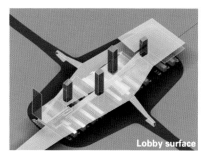

Lobby surface

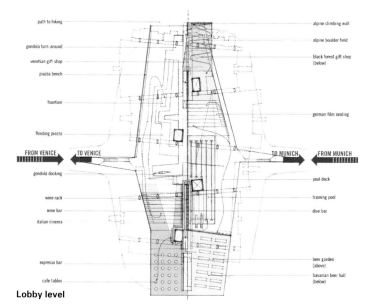

Elevator cores

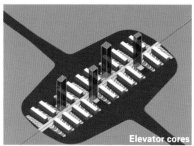

Bus parking

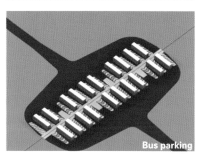

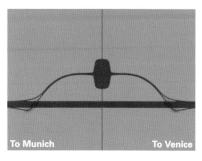

To Munich   To Venice

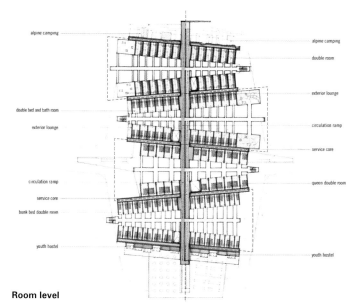

alpine camping

alpine camping
double room

double bed and bath room
exterior lounge

exterior lounge

circulation ramp

service core

circulation ramp
service core
bunk bed double room

queen double room

youth hostel

youth hostel

Room level

path to hiking

alpine climbing wall
gondola turn-around

alpine boulder field
venetian gift shop

black forest gift shop
piazza bench

(below)

fountain

german film seating
flooding piazza

FROM VENICE   **TO VENICE**   **TO MUNICH**   **FROM MUNICH**

gondola docking

pool deck
wine rack

training pool
wine bar

dive bar
italian cinema

expresso bar

beer garden

(above)
cafe tables

bavarian beer hall

(below)

Lobby level

loading zone

bus driver rooms
(above)

room-sized elevator
bus parking
bus unloading

room-sized elevator

check-out (to Venice)

check-in (from Munich)
check-in (from Venice)

check-out (to Munich)

room-sized elevator

bus unloading
room-sized elevator

bus parking

bus driver rooms
(above)

Parking Level

The hotel is a horizontal sandwich of six hotels that range in scale and amenity, echoing the differing economics of the tours offered. Each hotel bar is linked to the parking level with a single room-size elevator capable of holding a full busload of people. The hotel's individual corridors and room arrangements mirror the spatial logic of a bus's aisle and seats, while the open-air corridors flare toward the direction of travel.

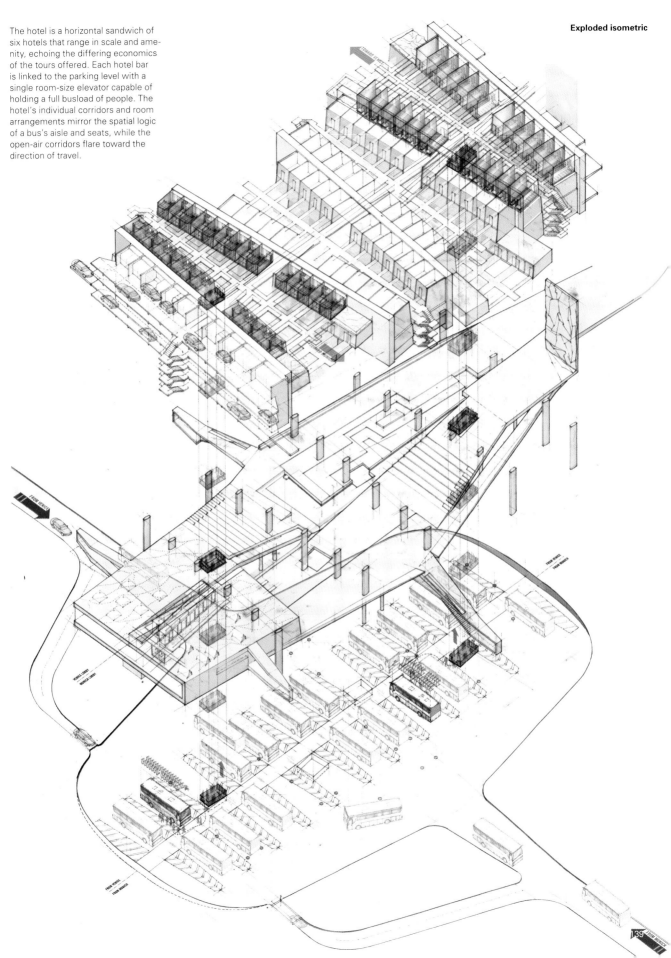

Installation from the exhibition New Hotel for Global Nomads

Visible from the access ramp, the elevation exhibits the building's unique organization. Joined into a single horizontal zone, the five hotel bars have open-air corridors, expanding in alternating directions, one toward Venice, the next toward Munich. The disparate ceiling heights of the hotel bars, indicative of different classes of accommodation, break up the mass of each bar. Structural spines support rows of rooms of adjacent hotel bars and contain the stacks of bathrooms. Linked to the social lobby underneath the hotel bars, the hotel's front desk functions like a tollbooth allowing registration by the busload.

The lowest floor is a bus parking garage, accessible from both sides of the highway, with buses aligned at their windshield, maintaining their orientation on the route.

Sectional model

LOBBY

BUS
-14'-0"

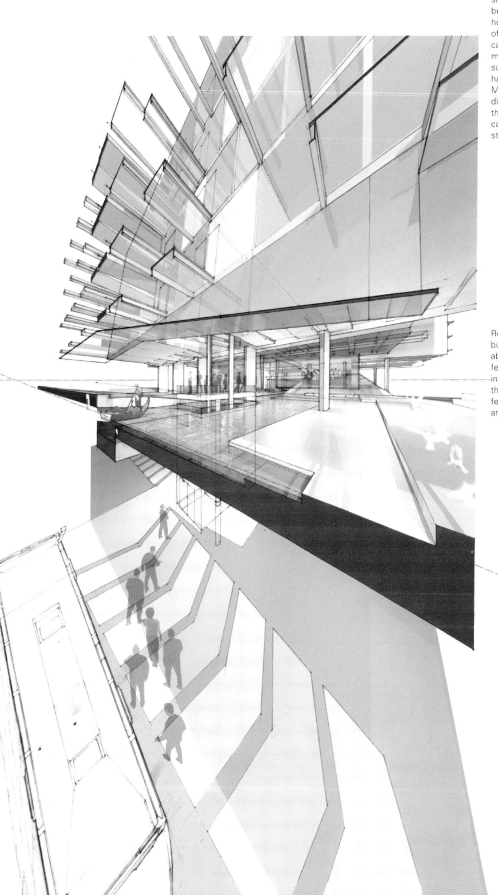

Part leisure landscape and part cruise ship deck, the open lobby located between the bus parking below and hotel bars above provides a series of collective programs—restaurants, cafes, pools, sports facilities, cinemas, and gift shops. This single surface is split down the middle, one half facing Venice, one facing Munich, with programs and activities divided according to orientation. In this way, for example, a wine bar and canal abut a beer hall and Olympic-style swimming pool.

Room-sized glass elevators link the bus parking level with the hotel bars above. Upon arrival, the elevator feeds directly to the hotel corridors, in the process sectioning through the social lobby complete with water features evocative of both Munich and Venice.

To maximize the floor area of the site, the individual double-loaded corridor hotels are joined at their bathrooms by a shared service wall, while their hallways are wedged open to become exterior spaces allowing light and air into each room.

The hotel bars are enclosed in a continuous glass skin that terminates in skylights that are placed underneath the building. As such, the underside of the building is its primary facade.

ROOM
+40'-0"

LOBBY

The outermost elevation of the hotel is reserved for automobile tourists, where room size is dictated by the size of the car and camping plots are available for low-budget travelers.

$

$$$

Plan perspective

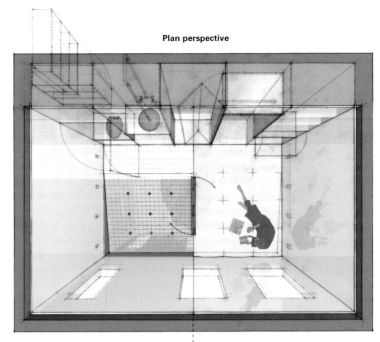

According to statistics, hotel inhabitants spend the majority of their time split between the bed and the bath. The Tourbus Hotel rooms are divided equally and only into a tiled bath surface and a soft bed surface. This tactic is varied to accommodate a variety of tourist classes that correspond to the economic ranges of the bus tours. Half the room is a continuous tiled surface that, when filled with water, serves as a large bathing pool, while the other half is as a continuous bed of resilient foam.

This distinction sets up a series of subsequent oppositions: hard/soft, wet/dry, hygiene/relaxation, etc. The softness of the bed side and the variable water level of the bath/pool produce multiple functional possibilities within a minimum of space—from casual lounging to sleep, from foot washing to full-body immersion.

Bath ┆ **Bed**

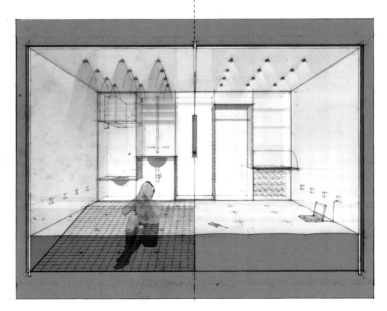

Sectional perspective

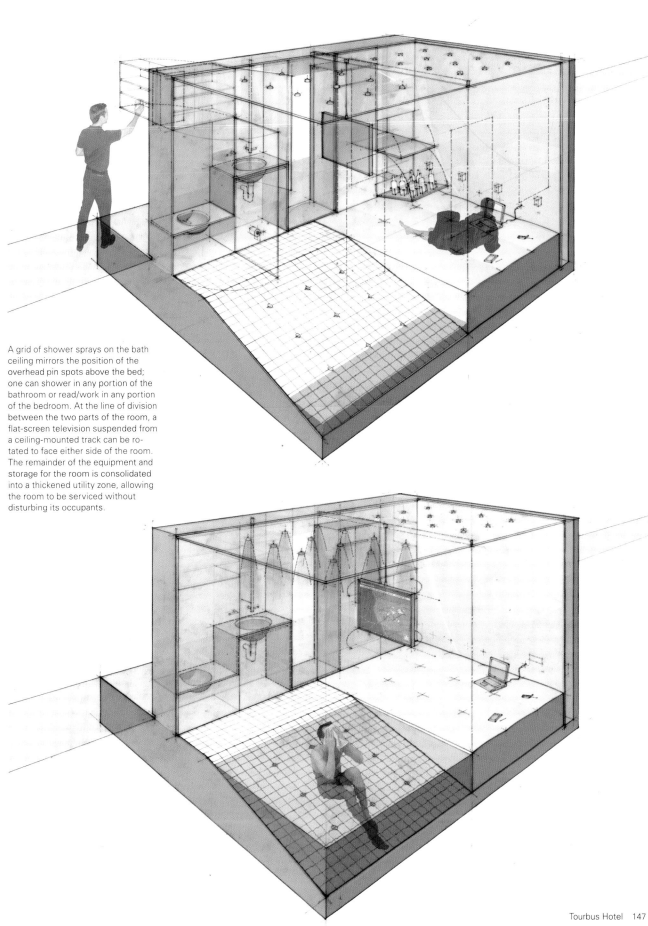

A grid of shower sprays on the bath ceiling mirrors the position of the overhead pin spots above the bed; one can shower in any portion of the bathroom or read/work in any portion of the bedroom. At the line of division between the two parts of the room, a flat-screen television suspended from a ceiling-mounted track can be rotated to face either side of the room. The remainder of the equipment and storage for the room is consolidated into a thickened utility zone, allowing the room to be serviced without disturbing its occupants.

Upside House

Prototypical American Suburb

This speculative house design was commissioned by Etekt.com, which attempted to pair clients with architects through parametric house design prototypes available on the internet. As such, the prototype had to be both general and specific, utopian and pragmatic, adjustable and fixed. Assuming the dimensions of a generic developer lot, the Upside House takes advantage of two opposed spatial logics of suburban space. The open-plan ground floor fulfills the modernist predilection for open space while the upper-floor plan is informed by a laundry list of private, commodity rooms—bedrooms, walk-in closets, master bathrooms, bonus rooms, etc.—required by the client.

While the relation of the Upside House to the street front remains constant, the number of bedrooms and other commodity rooms can be increased as desired by the client, which results in an equivalent spatial increase in the first-floor open-plan living below. As the house grows more spacious and more expensive, the slope of the stair becomes more gentle and gracious, ranging from the maximum allowable slope to a gradual angle ideal for protracted ceremonial descents.

The two floors of this suburban prototype are interconnected by a core, and the exterior is wrapped in a skin composed of a double envelope of translucent polycarbonate sheathing on conventional balloon frame construction.

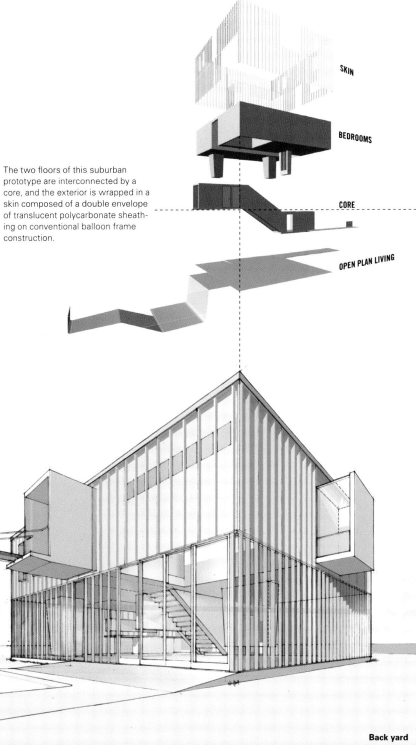

SKIN

BEDROOMS

CORE

OPEN PLAN LIVING

Back yard

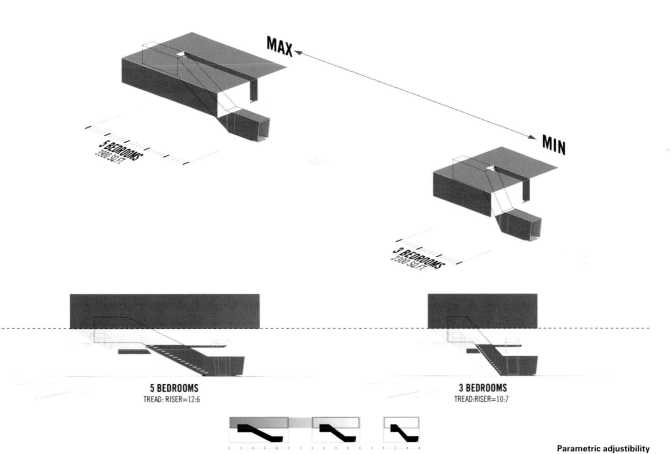

MAX

MIN

5 BEDROOMS
2900 SQ.FT.

3 BEDROOMS
2900 SQ.FT.

5 BEDROOMS
TREAD: RISER=12:6

3 BEDROOMS
TREAD:RISER=10:7

Parametric adjustibility

Front yard

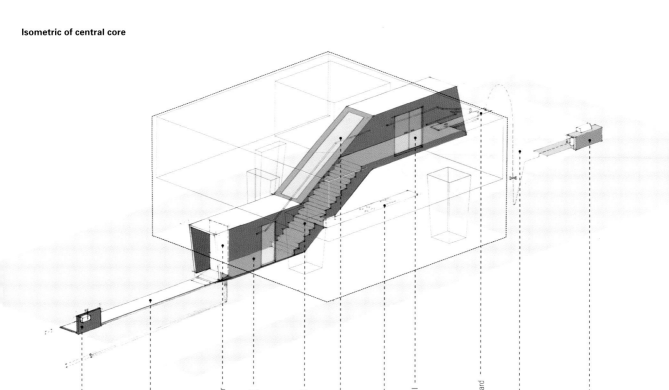

Mailbox ---- Sidewalk ---- Front door ---- Entry hall ---- Staircase ---- Skylight ---- Kitchen ---- Upper hall ---- Diving board ---- Pool ---- Grill

The core provides circulation and access to all spaces in the house and consolidates within a single element the essential iconographic features of the suburban dwelling: mailbox, porch, front door, central stair, kitchen, skylight, balcony/diving platform, and barbeque grill.

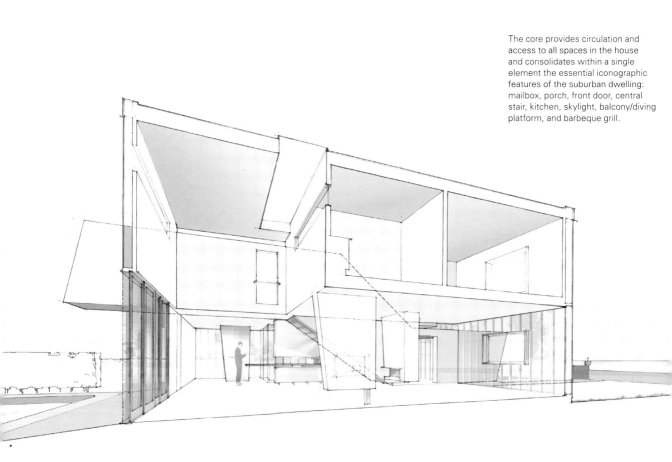

Sectional perspective

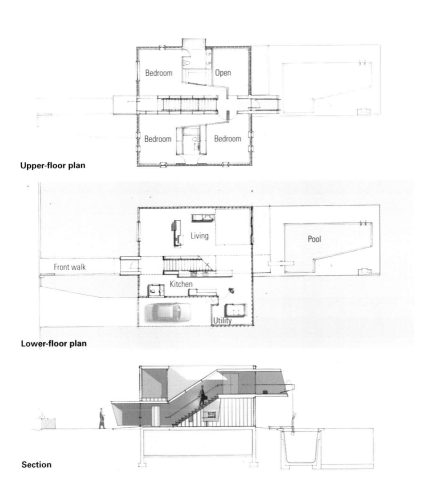

Upper-floor plan

Bedroom Open

Bedroom Bedroom

Lower-floor plan

Front walk

Living

Pool

Kitchen

Utility

Section

The desire for open-plan living is met on the ground floor where the plan is kept clear except for stalactite-like drop-downs from above. These interruptions in the first floor's open plan provide the necessary components for domestic living: fireplaces, audio/visual cabinets, stacked washer-dryers, and aquaria. Conversely, the solid mass of the upper story can be opened up below to provide double-height space for the entry hall, great room, etc. The number and nature of the drop-ins and cut-ups can be adjusted to suit the lifestyle of the individual client. As such, the membrane between the two floors can be manipulated for spatial and visual exchanges between private and public areas.

Open-plan living

Vegas 888 Spa and Skin

Las Vegas, Nevada

Increasingly, marketing and brand identity drive real estate and determine the success of high-profile projects. In the heated real-estate market of Las Vegas, the quest for a saleable image can determine form and alter content. LTL was called upon to strengthen the marketability of the Vegas 888 project, one of a multitude of high-rise condo towers in and around Las Vegas, through design, but their role began after the building had been schematically designed, its footprint determined, its structural grid set, and its overall floor plans and mechanical systems laid out. The design, restricted to a thin zone at the building's perimeter, maximized the effects of that skin, as both an advertising and architectural surface. On the 38th and 39th floors, LTL designed public leisure programs as a thickening of this skin; adjusting the organization of a spa, outdoor lounge, and bar area to magnify the economic, aesthetic, and optic potential of the building's surface.

In Las Vegas, where the color of glass becomes almost uncannily intense, in both the desert sun and the electricity-saturated night, the reflectivity and hue of a building can become its distinguishing iconic identity—MGM is green, Mandalay Bay is a specular gold. Accepting the modular economies of the curtain wall, LTL's options for revitalizing the exterior design of the building were limited to the inventive use of glass and color. Rather than utilizing a single tone, LTL conceived of the facade as a pixelated surface that shifts from a deep blue at the base to a lighter and more transparent hue and glazing at the crown.

advertising book by dbox

Unfolded skin

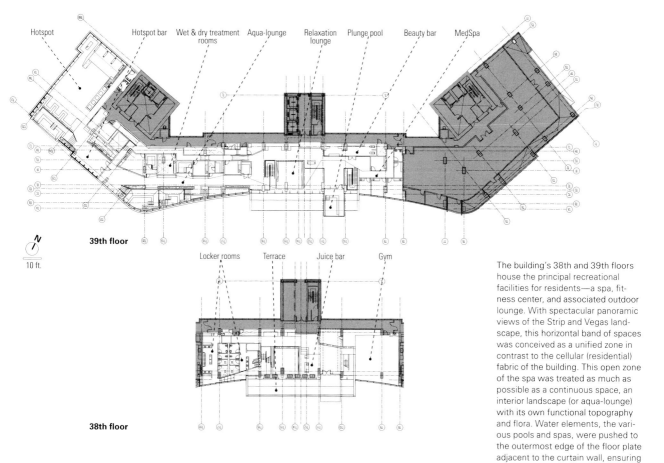

39th floor

Hotspot · Hotspot bar · Wet & dry treatment rooms · Aqua-lounge · Relaxation lounge · Plunge pool · Beauty bar · MedSpa

N
10 ft.

38th floor

Locker rooms · Terrace · Juice bar · Gym

The building's 38th and 39th floors house the principal recreational facilities for residents—a spa, fitness center, and associated outdoor lounge. With spectacular panoramic views of the Strip and Vegas landscape, this horizontal band of spaces was conceived as a unified zone in contrast to the cellular (residential) fabric of the building. This open zone of the spa was treated as much as possible as a continuous space, an interior landscape (or aqua-lounge) with its own functional topography and flora. Water elements, the various pools and spas, were pushed to the outermost edge of the floor plate adjacent to the curtain wall, ensuring optimal views and capitalizing on the extraordinary possibility of bathing 365 feet above the desert floor.

Panoramic perspective

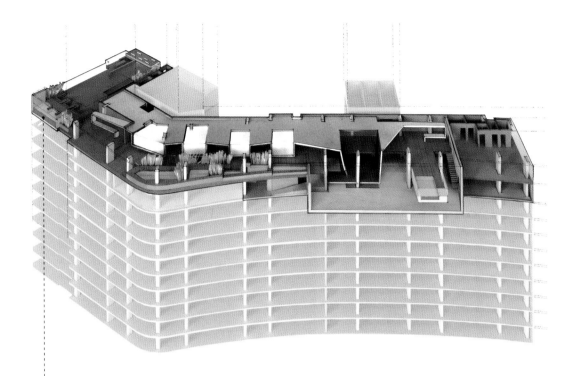

Hotspot

advertising book by dbox

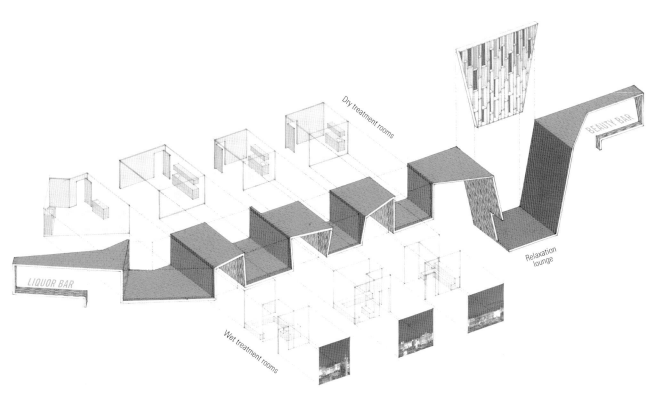

An undulating ribbon inserted into the aquatic landscape of the spa satisfies the need for enclosed treatment rooms. The ups and downs of the ribbon define private "dry" spaces (massage, aromatherapy, etc.) located in folds above the ribbon and more public "wet" rooms (saunas, showers, steam rooms) that occupy the spaces under the ribbon. The surfaces of the ribbon are clad in contrasting materials according to their function—cork for the dry interiors and tile for the wet spaces.

Section through wet/dry ribbon

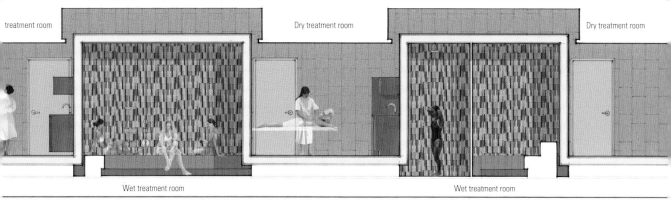

The Hotspot, located at the western edge of the 39th floor, extends the activities of the spa onto the roof terrace created by the building's set-back. A deck serves as a multi-functional surface, providing dance floor, private cabanas, sunbathing, and a skybar. A linear, collective pool forms one edge of the terrace abutting the building's curtain wall. Enfolded within the wing of an extended floor slab, the section of the pool is exposed as if cut by the building's edge. Utilizing shark-tank technology, a 16' plane of transparent acrylic forms one entire side of the pool, within which bathers float like tropical fish.

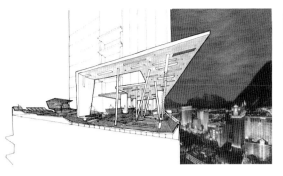

Hotspot sketch

Aqua-lounge sketch

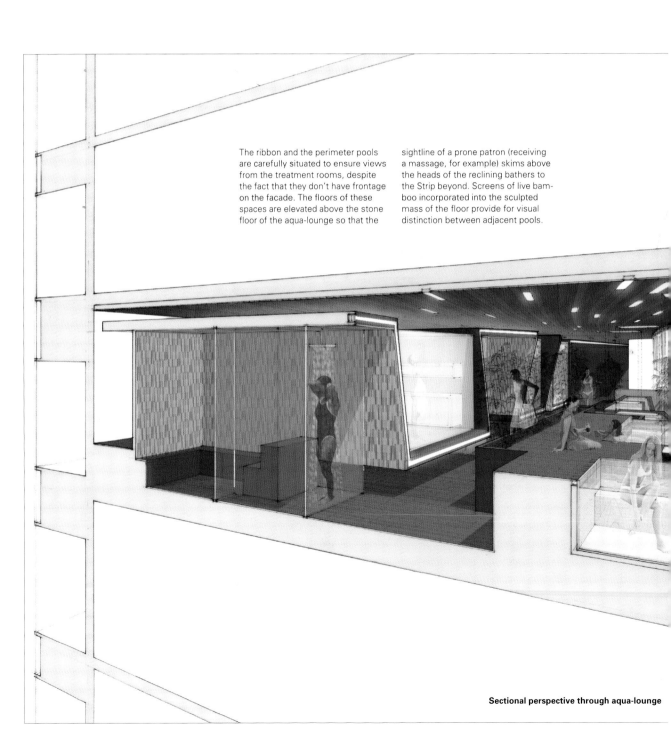

The ribbon and the perimeter pools are carefully situated to ensure views from the treatment rooms, despite the fact that they don't have frontage on the facade. The floors of these spaces are elevated above the stone floor of the aqua-lounge so that the sightline of a prone patron (receiving a massage, for example) skims above the heads of the reclining bathers to the Strip beyond. Screens of live bamboo incorporated into the sculpted mass of the floor provide for visual distinction between adjacent pools.

Sectional perspective through aqua-lounge

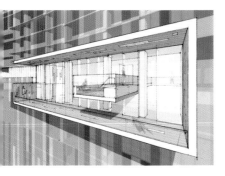

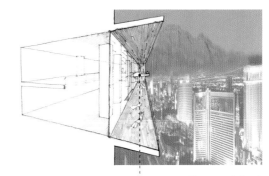

Plunge pool sketch

Plunge pool sketch

Projecting from the double-height entry space, a single plunge pool cantilevers off the face of the building. Suspended 40 stories above the landscape and lined with 2" acrylic panels, the pool offers the vertiginous pleasures of bathing in the unobstructed Vegas skyline.

advertising book by dbox

Wooster House

Wooster, Ohio

This renovation and addition to a 1950s house for an academic couple in Ohio began as a project to increase storage and space. To protect and celebrate the prairie-style qualities of the house, LTL's approach was one of selective local expansion. The project extends the horizontal spaces of the house into the surrounding landscape to form three new components: a living room deck, a new entry, and a library addition. Western red cedar cladding links the additions to the wood cladding and roof eaves of the original house.

Deck

Front entry

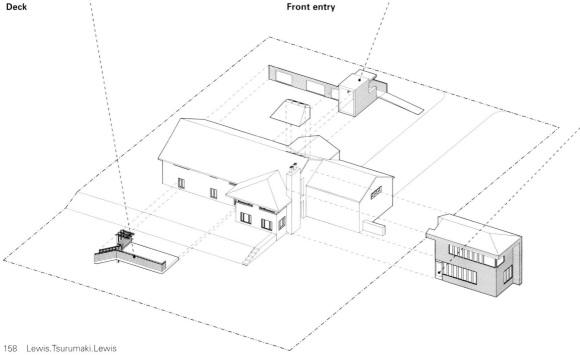

Library

The new library, the largest of these additions, was conceived as a single occupiable bookshelf that accommodates the extensive collections of the owners. The bookshelf wall joins lower and upper libraries, forming the spine of the new wing and providing a screen from the street. The sculpted form of this addition provides a roof profile for solar shading in the summer and allows light in during the winter.

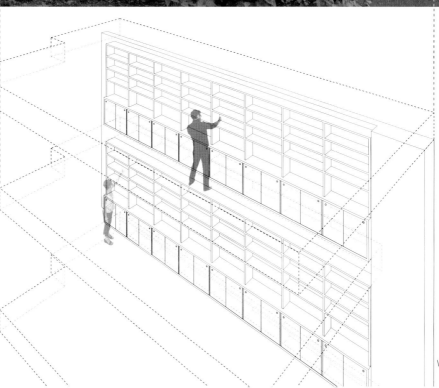

Xing Restaurant

New York, New York

This 2,000-square-foot Chinese restaurant occupies a floor plan typical of New York City residential buildings; light wells located on each side of the tenement building give it a dog-bone-like shape. Rather than hiding this distinctive narrowed section between the front and the back, LTL accentuated the unique nature of each of the spaces. Employing a logic derived from the Surrealist game—the Exquisite Corpse—LTL configured the four spaces into distinct yet interlocked areas.

Each of these areas is defined and wrapped by contrasting materials that shift from hard at the most public street entry to soft at the most private room in the back of the space. Stone marks the front bar area adjacent to the public entry. The bar counter is made from individual strips of translucent colored acrylic stacked on edge. This material extends up to serve as a light canopy that spans the front dining area; a room composed entirely of bamboo planks. The walls, steps, and ceiling of the next zone, a narrow corridor containing the

bathrooms and a wait station, are lined with the same stacked colored acrylic strips. The private dining room is enveloped by red velvet panels that turn this back room into an inhabitable padded booth, intentionally blurring the distinction between the space and the seats. At the thresholds between each of the four distinct areas, the materials' edges are expressed, calling attention to the role of the material as a thickened skin or shell.

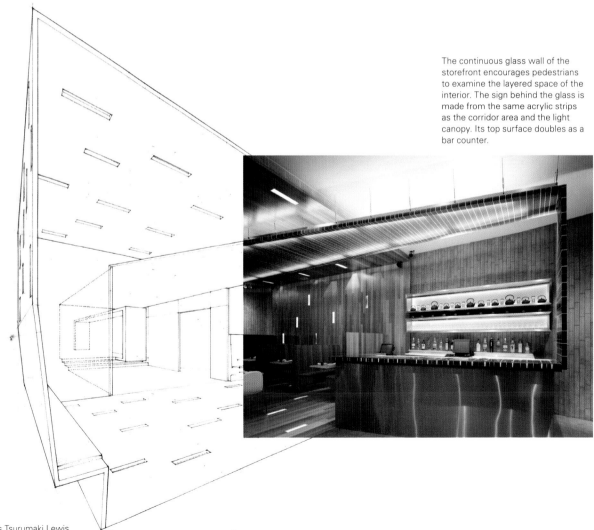

The continuous glass wall of the storefront encourages pedestrians to examine the layered space of the interior. The sign behind the glass is made from the same acrylic strips as the corridor area and the light canopy. Its top surface doubles as a bar counter.

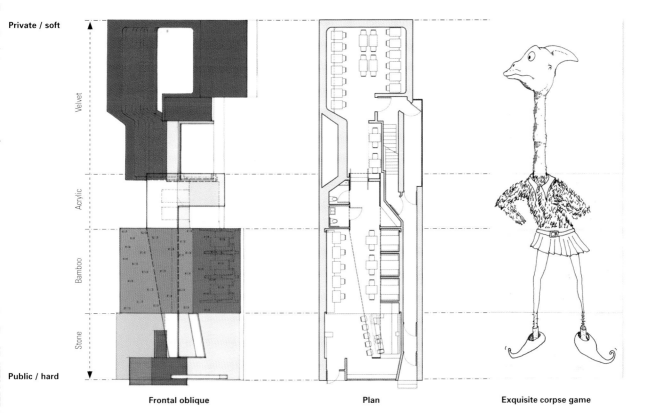

Private / soft

Velvet

Acrylic

Bamboo

Stone

Public / hard

Frontal oblique   Plan   Exquisite corpse game

Throughout the restaurant, lights are embedded in the materials, rather than designed as fixtures attached to walls or ceilings. These diffused lights tease out the richness and depth of the architectural surfaces. In the bamboo area, lights are placed within slots the width of the bamboo strips in the walls, ceiling, and floors. Dimmable linear incandescent lights line both sides of the acrylic canopy, allowing the acrylic walls and ceiling to glow at differing intensities.

The heart of the restaurant is also its service corridor, containing restrooms and a wait station. The walls, ceiling, and bathroom doors are all made from over 10,000 linear feet of stacked 1/4"-wide by 2"-deep acrylic strips. The ceiling canopy tapers from 8' at the restrooms to 2' at the bar, producing a forced perspective illusion of greater depth. The central corridor is animated by muted bathroom light transmitted through the acrylic walls; the diffused shadows of bathroom occupants play upon these surfaces.

In the private back dining area, the layered red velvet panels dissolve the distinction between enclosure and furniture as the banquette blends into the wall. The velvet also mutes ambient noise, increasing the intimacy of the room.

At the transition between the acrylic corridor and the red velvet room is lodged a 10-foot-long fish tank, whose surface is flush with the velvet padded panel. The fish tank provides soft illumination and fulfills the role of a window in an otherwise opaque wall.

Tactics for an Opportunistic Architecture

Toward an opportunistic architecture we propose five interwoven tactics. Retroactive, incomplete, and fragmented, they offer a partial list of possible trajectories for design. Rife with slippages and overlaps, they serve as means to a productive architectural practice.

Catalyzing Constraints

One of the principal tactics that underlies the work in this volume is the inverting of the value of constraints, by recasting the limitations of a project as the trigger for design invention. By maneuvering imaginatively within operational boundaries, the latent potentials of the project can be teased out of the very restrictions that would seem to weigh it down. In this sense, the seed for the most radical solution can always be found within the items that initially pose the greatest resistance. Rather than avoiding these obstacles through formal or logistical gymnastics, the tactic of catalyzing constraints generates an impassioned inquiry into the unavoidable limits of architectural production.

One means to come to terms with constraints is to selectively apply principles of efficiency in order to discover relationships through which the project can be pursued in unexpected, yet seemingly inevitable, ways. In general terms, efficiency is the coupling of a specific type of maximum to a particular minimum. In contemporary architectural discourse (and culture in general), efficiency is almost always assumed to be an economic equation, epitomized by the phrase: "maximizing profit for a minimum of cost." While such budgetary constraints are certainly significant factors in architectural practice, the singular emphasis on the bottom line in contemporary culture has rendered other forms of efficiency secondary and thus nearly unexamined. Rather than accepting the profit motive as the only determinant of efficiency, we propose an alternative approach: that efficiency be taken as a self-consciously nurtured catalyst, setting in motion a playful exchange between two interrelated constraints.

Other well-known efficiencies play this out in more interesting, albeit still expected, ways: structural efficiency seeks to maximize stability with minimal material obligation; spatial efficiency seeks to maximize utility with a minimal amount of square footage, and so on. However, what if the efficiencies were more constructive or elective? These unexpected pairings could set in motion a process which would be at once inevitable relative to the logics at hand, but no longer driven by singular pragmatic or rational outcomes. An efficiency based on maximizing daylight, for instance, could result in an intricately distorted ceiling produced by the study of solar angles, or attempts to minimize points of structural contact with a complex plane and maximize spans could result in an ingenious interplay between structure and form. In these examples there is a recognition that efficiency applied in one way can often generate extreme inefficiency or even exorbitance in other dimensions.

The five projects for restaurants demonstrate an attempt to exploit constraints through intensified efficiencies. In all of these instances the site consisted of a predetermined space within an existing building—an envelope with defined planimetric and dimensional limits. Due to the restrictions of these spaces, the plan, territory that usually provides the most fertile ground for architectural operation, was largely predetermined by the imperative to maximize seating and accommodate adequate circulation and service space. The obligation to provide a spatially efficient plan meant that the focus of design invention was shifted to the surfaces of the walls and ceilings, requiring these often under-considered elements to take on a greater architectural vitality. Instead of simply applying materials to the existing envelope, each of these projects involves the insertion of a new volume, calibrated to the performative requirements of the program, within the first. By treating this liminal zone as a thickened, composite membrane, these projects became the testing grounds for the reinvention of the architectural surface. In these cases the strict adherence to planimetric efficiency compels an intensified investigation into maximizing the possibilities—material and programmatic—of the interior skin of each space.

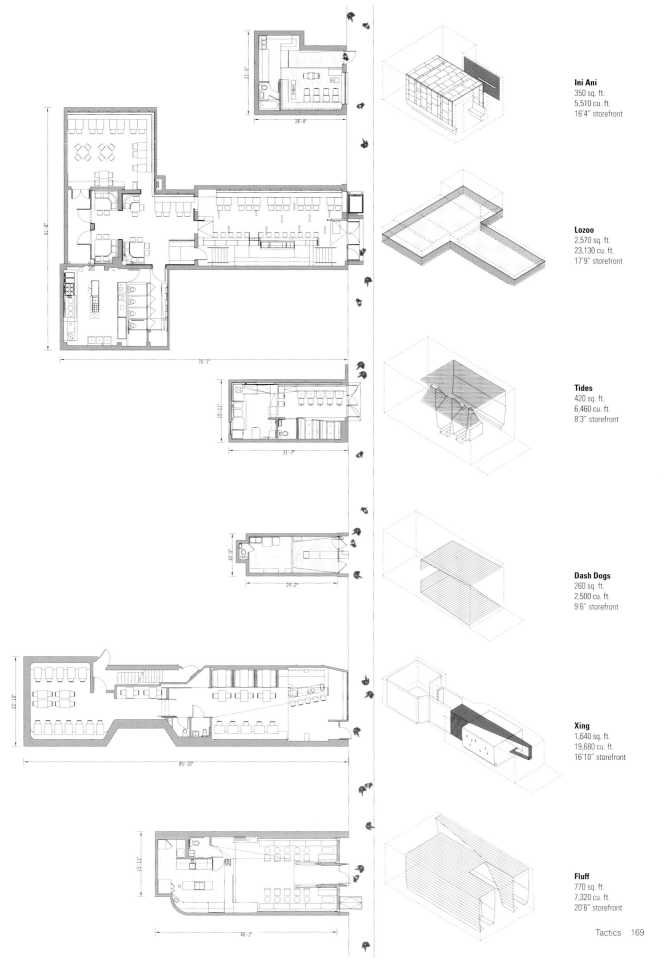

Ini Ani
350 sq. ft.
5,510 cu. ft.
16'4" storefront

Lozoo
2,570 sq. ft.
23,130 cu. ft.
17'9" storefront

Tides
420 sq. ft.
6,460 cu. ft.
8'3" storefront

Dash Dogs
260 sq. ft.
2,500 cu. ft.
9'6" storefront

Xing
1,640 sq. ft.
19,680 cu. ft.
16'10" storefront

Fluff
770 sq. ft.
7,320 cu. ft.
20'6" storefront

Invention Sprawl

While there have been several attempts to apply the principles of Surrealism (as an artistic and literary movement) to architecture, a more productive line of inquiry may be derived from Gaston Bachelard's related concept—Surrationalism. Surrationalism is a conscious, critical, and rational process that, unlike the Surrealist interest in the irrational aspects of the unconscious, rigorously applies logic to the limits of rationality itself. Tactically this means pursuing a particular set of logics to the breaking point—the point at which they fold back upon themselves and the line between the rational and the absurd becomes blurred.

This pattern of inquiry, as applied to the projects in this book, can be termed "invention sprawl." Rather than a linear process derived from a narrow interpretation of the scientific method that either confirms or denies a priori expectations, invention sprawl requires a more fluid process of research, where the close examination of a subject opens new areas for investigation, which in turn set forth a logic of inquiry, again opening new areas, and so on. The resultant cumulative knowledge cannot be anticipated by the starting point. Here, the desire for a singular answer is suspended and the line of research is no longer obligated to confirm predicted outcomes. In this way, the rational trajectories of the architectural project are opened up to unexpected results, extrapolated to the point that they produce a precipitate of paradoxical effects and surrational possibilities.

An example of invention sprawl is Angelo Invernizzi's 1935 Villa Girasole located outside of Verona. A simple desire—to maximize the house's exposure to sunlight—produced an intricate sequence of rational decisions resulting in a quixotic, if not illogical, whole. In order to maintain optimal solar orientation over the course of the day, the house rotates on a massive turntable supported by fifteen train wheels. With the push of a button, a series of low horsepower motors slowly move the platform, enabling the house to be kept in perfect alignment with the sun as it crosses the sky. This mechanical contrivance—eminently logical given the initial premise—triggers a series of repercussive effects.

As a result of the rotation, the house is split in two: a mobile upper portion supported by a heavy stone base that serves as the fixed point of access. Where the base is solid and traditional (designed by architect Ettore Fagiuoli), the rotating section is machine-like and ephemeral (designed by the owner-engineer, Invernizzi), constructed of a light-weight concrete frame infilled with straw to reduce loads and skinned in gleaming sheets of metal. The two divergent halves form an architectural exquisite corpse, joined at a garden whose geometry inscribes the path of movement and pinned together by the circular stair and elevator core. The stair core spins with the upper house while extending into the base to terminate in a subterranean wine cellar—vertical circulation is coupled with rotational movement. The elevator moves in three directions—up, down, and around while staying centered in plan.

The upper house contains the principal living spaces. The most banal domestic functions are here distorted according to the demands of mobility. Plumbing and furniture have to be rethought: sewer and water connections are made through pipes into holding tanks slung from the underside of the house—the architectural equivalent of colostomy bags—while storage and cabinetry are built into the walls to reduce loading to the rotating frame. The need to balance the weight across the platform produces an uncanny doubling of space, with mirror-image plans that generate redundant rooms.

The logic of the inquiry—tethering architecture to the movement of the sun—destabilizes and inverts the assumed fixed relationship between building and site. Expected distinctions between front, back, and side yards no longer apply—the terrace can orient to the distant view to the south or connect to the rear grounds to the north. Doors may open onto different places at different times of day. From a vantage point within the house, the surrounding vineyards seem to rotate around the architecture, transforming the perception of the landscape from a series of static, picturesque views into a slow but continuous panorama. The sun can rise and fall in the same window. The house can arrest shadows and warp the perception of time.

While not the intent of its designers, Villa Girasole, an irrational product of rational objectives, maps the process and pleasures of invention sprawl.

Maximize solar exposure

Paradoxical Pleasures

In the modernist paradigm, rational systems of organization and definitive distinctions hold sway. A constructed order is imposed on the messy and multiform reality of the everyday, and architecture is expected to hold in check otherwise fluid or blurred conditions. In articulating clear distinctions between contrasting phenomena—between interior and exterior, functional and decorative, structure and enclosure, served and service, sacred and profane, etc.—architecture tends to naturalize and enhance these differences even as it attempts to link them into coherent patterns. Rather than seeking a seamless resolution of complex and often contradictory conditions, many of our projects playfully amplify the paradoxical and often absurd conditions that architecture is called upon to prop up or hold in check.

Emblematic of this tactic is the Exquisite Corpse, a Surrealist game in which a single sheet of paper is folded into four segments, each corresponding to a portion of the body (head, torso, legs, and feet). Each part of the figure is drawn by a different participant without knowledge of the form of the adjacent parts. The device of the fold-line allows for the coexistence of contradictory conditions that nevertheless must conform to an overall anthropomorphic logic (head links to body, and so on). The focus on the fold-line here is on the amplification of its artificiality and on the way in which it allows for the production of an irrationally logical result. Xing Restaurant exemplifies this technique, revealing how the logic of the exquisite corpse intensifies local difference in the service of a more seductive whole.

Similarly, several of our projects exploit the effect of a datum to foreground and intensify distinctions, encourage slippages between binary conditions, and provoke interaction among seemingly disparate elements. In the simplest form this involves the precise materialization of the line as a site of contestation and negotiation where conflicting elements adjoin along an infinitesimal edge, as in the juxtaposition of new and old in the Geltner Loft or the horizontal delineation that binds spaces in Lozoo Restaurant. These tactics operate by foregrounding the line between oppositional conditions—thereby rendering explicit architecture's role in the construction of these differences.

In other cases, seemingly contradictory conditions are intentionally brought into contact and made to engage one another. Architectural components which are typically conceived of as oppositional are forced to enter into a productive exchange, often shifting roles and identities in the process. In our proposal for the Great Egyptian Museum, it is the interference between ground and sky, between the roof plane and the ground plane, that generates the programmatic and spatial interest of the project. The solar canopy drops down to form a series of diverse relationships with the extruded landscape pylons, alternately performing as window, display wall, vitrine, or structural courtyard, while the pylons' repetitive forms are coded and differentiated by these engagements.

It is not, however, the formal technique—whether folding, cutting, or extrusion—that provides interest, but rather the ways that these manipulations produce new relationships between uses, confound hierarchies, and liberate unexamined possibilities within known programs. These slippings, pullings, and distortions can lead to new productive couplings (New Suburbanism, Upside House), hold contrasting conditions in a charged proximity (Vegas 888, Building 82%), or play with recognizable distinctions between entrance and exit (Dash Dogs) or memory and anticipation (Tourbus Hotel).

Horizontal split ----

Vertical split ----

Push you pull me --

Exquisite corpse ---

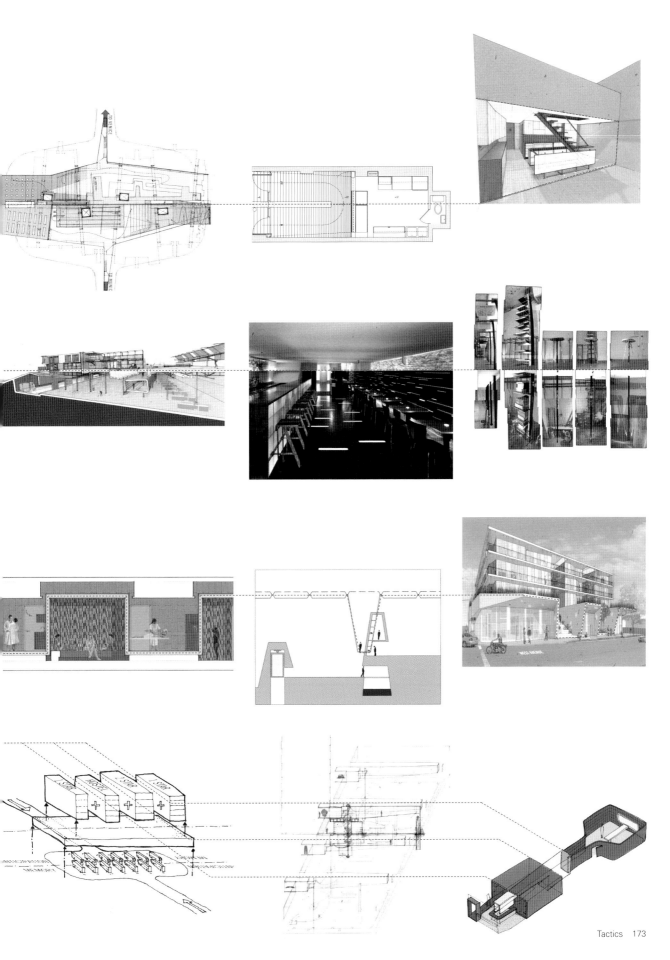

18,500 linear feet of felt and plywood strips

Alchemical Assemblies

A common technique in comedy is the use of repetition. A carefully repeated phrase can transform material from the banal to the delightful. These shifts in perception and meaning are fascinating, drawing on the power of choreographed repetition to render ordinary language (the original phrase or word) disproportionately humorous. To repeat a well-known epigram, quantity has a quality of its own.

In several of the projects in this volume, the possibilities of repetition as an architectural technique are explored. The quantity can be material (25,000 strips of cardboard in Ini Ani), programmatic (34 floors of intertwined parking and program in Park Tower) or performative (the continuous repetition of mechanized movement in Bellow or Refiled). In each case, the visual, physical, and conceptual effects of these dense assemblies are more compelling and less predictable than the quantity itself.

For example, in the case of material repetition, inexpensive and readily available materials are aggregated to produce complex composite surfaces. The rich spatial and visual qualities of these assemblies belie their prosaic origins. In Tides, common bamboo skewers produce a spatially dynamic topographical ceiling. Miles of felt and plywood strips induce both sensations of speed and stasis in Fluff Bakery. In Ini Ani, a wall of plaster-cast coffee lids displays the taxonomy of an everyday object, yet reads as an unfamiliar pattern from a distance.

Whereas architects are typically removed from the production of surfaces and materials, relegated to specifying predetermined products and systems, the assemblies in these projects employ the excessive repetition of inexpensive materials and prosaic objects to re-invigorate the potential of the surface. Instead of relying on expensive materials applied in predictable ways, these practices deploy common materials in unusual ways.

The resulting explorations of optical patterns and tactile qualities induce a perceptual oscillation between the individual component and the overall field, wherein the singular qualities of the isolated object result in unforeseen and contrasting effects. Seen up close, the part retains its autonomy, while seen from a distance, the fluctuations and variations within the whole gain dominance.

Assembly

Surface

Space

2,378 air fresheners

479 coffee-cup lids

110,000 bamboo skewers

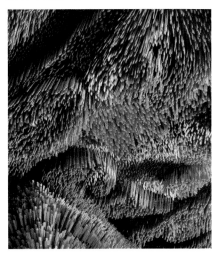

Over Drawing

In Balzac's novel *The Unknown Master-piece* the protagonist, Porbus, struggles to unite two styles of painting that have split the discourse of art, best illustrated in the debate between Ingres and Delacroix. On Ingres's side are those who argue that art and representation is a demonstration of the intellect and as such should be controlled and conveyed through line, drawing or *disegno*. The supporters of Delacroix argue that the purpose of art is the translation of the world through the effects of paint, engulfing the viewer in the totality of the image through color or *colorito*. Whether told as the contest of Michelangelo versus Titian, Rome versus Venice, line versus color, or thought versus passion, the central tenets of the debate remain the same.

While Balzac's Porbus ultimately overcomes the dichotomy through masterful synthesis, over 150 years later the discourse of architecture is repeating this debate, now cast into the arena of technology and representation. Because of its dependence on line and delineation to control the translation of ideas into built form, the discipline of architecture has almost always sided with Ingres, Michelangelo, and *disegno*. However, with the introduction of digital technology—specifically, complex rendering software that can situate the viewer within an atmospheric and perceptually realistic representation of space—the possibility for reviving the argument of Delacroix, Titian, and *colorito* has emerged, and with vengeance.

Unfortunately, this has resulted in a tedious and counterproductive split between proponents of traditional forms of architectural representation (drawing by hand, sketching, and hardline constructions) who claim the inherent intellectual value of drawing as a means to knowledge, and those who favor digitally generated immersive representations (generated through high-end, complex, and often expensive programs) and tend to see past techniques as antiquated.

Recognizing the simultaneous potential and limitation of both approaches, we seek to cultivate and encourage a Porbus-like search for a truly complex form of architectural representation, one that learns from both, steals selectively, and pays little heed to zealots on either side. This means inventing drafting, representational, and production tactics that short-circuit traditional protocols and patterns of work determined largely by software constraints. It calls for an agile exchange between line and color, between drawing and production, between manual and digital means of working in order to circumvent current frames of thinking for the benefit of continuing architectural vitality.

The drawings in this book combine what works best from the overlaps of disparate mediums and methods, through an active looping exchange between scanners, printers, software, and parallel rules. Color, tone, and surface qualities from digital renderings integrate with lines, edges, and details from 3H leads on 4mm Mylar. The speed of one is augmented (and slowed down) by the agility of the other. Rather than relying on a single technique, rapid computer-generated renderings are overdrawn by hand, with detailed development and design alterations to the initial form emerging in the process. These drawings are then scanned and recomposed with the original rendering, and this hybrid image is further digitally manipulated to capitalize on the qualities of both media.

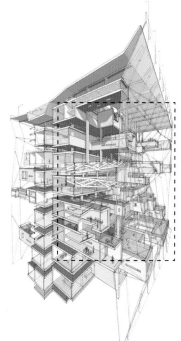

3H lead drawing on 4mm Mylar

Drawing parts added digitally

Digital rendering

Digital integration

Digital manipulation

Digital manipulation

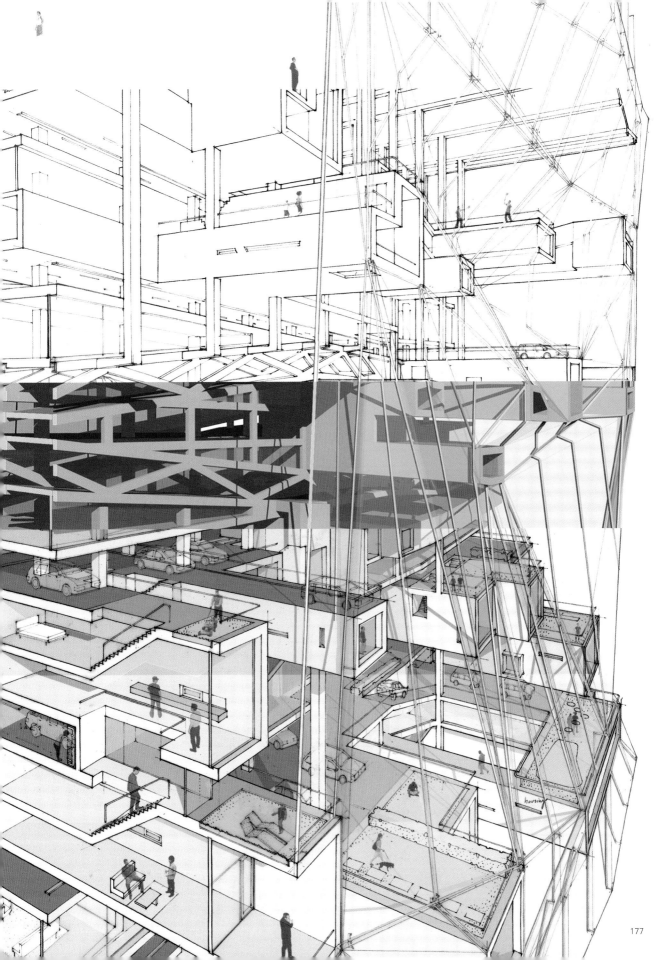

Project Credits

Slip Space Installation, 1994, Storefront for Art and Architecture, New York, NY --------------
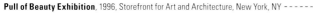
Client: Storefront for Art and Architecture
Collaborator: Peter Pelsinski
Curators: Beatriz Colomina, Dennis Dollens, Eve Kosofsky Sedgwick, Henry Urbach, Cindi Patton,
   Mark Wigley
Gallery co-directors: Shirin Neshat and Kyong Park
Project team: Paul Lewis, Marc Tsurumaki, David J. Lewis

Pull of Beauty Exhibition, 1996, Storefront for Art and Architecture, New York, NY ------------------
Client: Storefront for Art and Architecture
Collaborator: Peter Pelsinski
Curators: Victoria Milne and Kiki Smith
Gallery co-directors: Shirin Neshat and Kyong Park
Project team: Paul Lewis, Marc Tsurumaki, David J. Lewis
Installation team: Karen Stonely, Carmen Lenzi, Joanne Liou, Nicholas Tobier, Hilary Sample,
   Michael Meredith, Stephanie Baffler, Kim Yao
Metal fabrication: Veyko
Wood fabrication: Robert Kulka

Eavesdropping Installation, 1996, Exit Art/ The First World, New York, NY -----------------------
Client: Exit Art / The First World, NYC
Gallery co-directors/curators: Jeanette Ingberman and Papo Colo
Project team: Paul Lewis, Marc Tsurumaki, David J. Lewis
Installation team: Chris Korsh, Mark Shephard, Bill Peterson, David Ruff, Jennifer Whitburn,
   Clarissa Richardson, Kim Yao
Photographer: Michael Moran

Skyfill Landfill Speculative Project, 1996
Client: Van Alen Institute Competition for Governors Island
Project Team: Paul Lewis, Marc Tsurumaki, David J. Lewis

Testing 1...2...3... Exhibition, 1997, Storefront for Art and Architecture, New York, NY ------
Client: Storefront for Art and Architecture
Gallery co-directors: Shirin Neshat and Kyong Park
Project team: Paul Lewis, Marc Tsurumaki, David J. Lewis; Deane Simpson, project manager
Installation team: Patrice Gardera, Rachel Grey, Janette Kim, Carmen Lenzi, Lynn Sullivan,
   Alexandra Ultsch, Kim Yao, Christine Kolovich

Container Building Speculative Project, 1997
Project team: Paul Lewis, Marc Tsurumaki, David J. Lewis

Exquisite Corpse Clothing Store Speculative Project, 1997
Project team: Paul Lewis, Marc Tsurumaki, David J. Lewis

Free Lobby / Block 1290 Speculative Project, 1997
Project team: Paul Lewis, Marc Tsurumaki, David J. Lewis

Mies-on-a-beam Speculative Project, 1997
Project team: Paul Lewis, Marc Tsurumaki, David J. Lewis

Sportbars Speculative Project, 1997
Project team: Paul Lewis, Marc Tsurumaki, David J. Lewis

Video/Filmplex Speculative Project, 1997
Project team: Paul Lewis, Marc Tsurumaki, David J. Lewis

Mantel Piece Installation, 1997, Young Architects Forum Exhibition, Urban Center Galleries, New York, NY -----------------
Client: The Architectural League of New York
Project team: Paul Lewis, Marc Tsurumaki, David J. Lewis

Van Alen Institute, 1998, New York, NY --

Client: Van Alen Institute
Project team: Paul Lewis, Marc Tsurumaki, David J. Lewis; Troy Ostrander, Neil Henk,
   Michael Meredith, Jeff Etelamaki, Philip Shearer, Lee Jung Hong
Contractor: Marcelino Magaan Jr.
Reception desk fabrication: Veyko

Princeton Architectural Press Offices, 1997–98, New York, NY - - - - - - - - - - - - - - - -
Client: Princeton Architectural Press
Project team: Paul Lewis, Marc Tsurumaki, David J. Lewis; Troy Ostrander, Mari Fujita

Happy Mazza Media Company Offices, 1998, New York, NY -
Client: Happy Mazza Media Company
Project team: Paul Lewis, Marc Tsurumaki, David J. Lewis; Lee Jung Hong, Phillip Shearer, Neil Henk, Michael Meredith
Contractor: Vast King Corporation

Everest Partners LLC Offices, 1999, New York, NY
Client: Everest Partners, LLC
Project team: Paul Lewis, Marc Tsurumaki, David J. Lewis; Troy Ostrander
Contractor: Interior Building Services

Carson Apartment, 1999, New York, NY
Client: Heather Carson
Project team: Paul Lewis, Marc Tsurumaki, David J. Lewis
Contractor: Vast King Corporation

Alexakos House, 2000, Southampton, NY -
Client: Constantine Alexakos
Project team: Paul Lewis, Marc Tsurumaki, David J. Lewis; David Takacs,
    Lucas Cascardo, Mike Johnston, Stephanie Tuerk
Contractor: Sand Pebble Builders Inc., Oscar Mejias
Metal fabrication: Veyko

Geltner Loft, 1999–2000, New York, NY -
Client: Danita Geltner
Project team: Paul Lewis, Marc Tsurumaki, David J. Lewis; David Takacs, Jason Tang
Contractor: IJ Universal

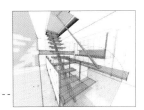

Refiled Installation, 2000, National Design Triennial, The Cooper-Hewitt National Design Museum, New York, NY - - - - - - - - -
Client: The Cooper-Hewitt National Design Museum, Smithsonian Institution
Curators: Donald Albrecht, Ellen Lupton, Steven Skov Holt
Project team: Paul Lewis, Marc Tsurumaki, David J. Lewis; Troy Ostrander, Ronald De Villa, Eunice Seng,
    Makram El-Kadi, Naji Moujaes, Carmen Lenzi, Michelle Lenzi
Support provided by: Cornell University, Parsons The New School for Design, Mercedes T. Bass Rome Prize in
    Architecture from The American Academy in Rome

New Suburbanism Speculative Project, 2000
Project team: Paul Lewis, Marc Tsurumaki, David J. Lewis; Michael Tyre, Hye-Young Chung, Jason Tang

10 Shades of Green Exhibition, 2000, Urban Center Galleries, The Architectural League, New York, NY - - - - - - -
Client: The Architectural League of New York
Curator: Peter Buchanan
Project director: Rosalie Genevro
Exhibition coordinator: Andrew Blum
Project development: Gregory Wessner
Project team: Paul Lewis, Marc Tsurumaki, David J. Lewis
Installation team: Troy Ostrander; Gia Wolff, Judith Tse, Carla Munoz-Puente, Brendan Lee, Damian Jackson,
    Emily Abruzzo, Miko Smith, Christine Kang, Alex Chan, Herbin Ng, model makers
Display tables fabrication: Veyko
Introductory text graphics: Tricia Solsaa
Photographer: Michael Moran

Essex Street Studios, 2001, New York, NY -
Collaborator: Freecell
Project team: Paul Lewis, Marc Tsurumaki, David J. Lewis; Clement Valla, Hye-Young Chung, Mathan Ratinan,
    Damian Jackson

The Architectural League of New York Offices, 2001, New York, NY
Client: The Architectural League of New York
Project team: Paul Lewis, Marc Tsurumaki, David J. Lewis; David Takacs, project architect; Hye-Young Chung,
    Clement Valla

Upside House, 2001
Client: www.Etekt.com
Project team: Paul Lewis, Marc Tsurumaki, David J. Lewis; Phillip Speranza

Architecture + Water Exhibition, 2001, Van Alen Institute, New York, NY
Client: Van Alen Institute
Curators: Paul Lewis, Marc Tsurumaki, David J. Lewis
Project team: Paul Lewis, Marc Tsurumaki, David J. Lewis; Troy Ostrander, David Takacs, Kevin Oliver,
    Hye-Young Chung, Garrick Ambrose, Erik Gerlach, Young-Hye Yoo

Prototype Hotel Room, 2001, Fremont Hotel, San Francisco, CA
Commissioned by: *Interiors Magazine*
Collaborators: L.E.FT
Project team: Paul Lewis, Marc Tsurumaki, David J. Lewis

Lozoo Restaurant, 2000–2, New York, NY
Client: Greg Kan and Li Ping
Project team: Paul Lewis, Marc Tsurumaki, David J. Lewis; David Takacs, project architect; Hye-Young Chung,
    Clement Valla, Stephanie Tuerk, Malene Holmsgaard
Mechanical engineer: Mottola Rini Engineers
Structural engineer: Chen Engineering
Contractor: Yellow Square
Mirror fabrication: Veyko
Photographer: Michael Moran

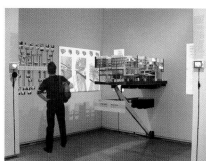

Davies Penthouse, 2002, New York, NY
Client: Peter N. C. Davies
Project team: Paul Lewis, Marc Tsurumaki, David J. Lewis; Carolynn Karp, David Takacs, Clement Valla
Structural engineer: Robert Silman Associates
Mechanical engineer: Mottola Rini Engineers

Great Egyptian Museum Competition, 2002, Giza, Egypt
Competition sponsor: The Arab Republic of Egypt, Ministry of Culture, Supreme Council of Antiquities
Project team: Paul Lewis, Marc Tsurumaki, David J. Lewis; Roman Torres, Christian Munoz, Ebby Wise Carver,
    Hye-Young Chung

Tourbus Hotel Speculative Project, 1999–2002, in New Hotels for Global Nomads exhibition,
    Cooper-Hewitt National Design Museum, New York, NY
Curator: Donald Albrecht
Project team: Paul Lewis, Marc Tsurumaki, David J. Lewis; Hye-Young Chung, project manager;
    Jake Nishimura, Ade Herkarisma, Jamie Montgomery, Larry Cohn, David Takacs, Eric Samuels
Support provided by: Mercedes T. Bass Rome Prize in Architecture from The American Academy in Rome

Wooster House, 2001–3, Wooster, OH
Client: Susan and Richard Figge
Project team: Paul Lewis, Marc Tsurumaki, David J. Lewis; Hye-Young Chung, Phillip Speranza, Stephanie Tuerk
Contractor: Suttle Construction
Landscaping: E.F. Pouly Company
Photographer: Michael Moran

FAAR-Out Exhibition: Six Months in Rome, 2003, The Art Directors Club, New York, NY
Curators: Linda Blumberg, Myrna Davis, Sarah Hartman
Project team: Paul Lewis, Marc Tsurumaki, David J. Lewis; Hye-Young Chung, project manager
Installation team: David Takacs, Eric Samuels, Bethany Martin, Mark Thorpe, Michelle Leong

Light Structures Display Device, 2003
Project team: Paul Lewis, Marc Tsurumaki, David J. Lewis; Hye-Young Chung, David Takacs, Clement Valla

Perth Amboy High School Competition, 2003, Perth Amboy, NJ
Client: Perth Amboy High School
Project team: Paul Lewis, Marc Tsurumaki, David J. Lewis; Eric Samuels, Sima Rustom, Hilary Zaic,
    Joshua Weiselberg

World Trade Center Memorial Competition, 2003, Ground Zero, New York, NY
Competition sponsor: Lower Manhattan Development Corporation
Project team: Paul Lewis, Marc Tsurumaki, David J. Lewis; Eric Samuels, Sima Rustom, Joshua Weiselberg

Bornhuetter Hall, 2001–4, The College of Wooster, Wooster, OH
Client: The College of Wooster
Project team: Paul Lewis, Marc Tsurumaki, David J. Lewis; David Takacs, project architect; Hye-Young Chung,
    Carolynn Karp, Eric Samuels, Clement Valla, Stephanie Tuerk, Patri Vienravi

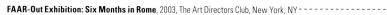

Construction manager: Bogner Construction Management Company
Structural engineer: Robert Silman Associates
Mechanical engineer: Point One Design
Photographer: Rudolph Janu, Michael Moran

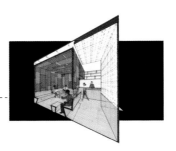

Ini Ani Coffee Shop, 2004, New York, NY -
Client: Kevin Mancini and Payam Yazdani
Project team: Paul Lewis, Marc Tsurumaki, David J. Lewis; James Bennett, Lucas Cascardo, Alex Terzich
Contractor: J. Z. Interior Renovations
Photographer: Michael Moran

Rotare Light, 2003–4 -
Client: Ivalo Lighting Incorporated
Project Team: Paul Lewis, Marc Tsurumaki, David J. Lewis; Eric Samuels

Seward Park Lobby Competition, 2004, Lower East Side, New York, NY - - - - - - - - - - - - - -
Client: Seward Park Housing Corporation
Project team: Paul Lewis, Marc Tsurumaki, David J. Lewis; Lucas Cascardo, project architect; Hilary Zaic,
    James Bennett
Structural Engineer: Robert Silman Associates

Parking Sections Installation, 2004, U.S. Pavilion, Venice Biennale, 9th International Architecture Exhibition
Curators: *Architectural Record*, Robert Ivy, Clifford Pearson, Suzanne Stephens
Project team: Paul Lewis, Marc Tsurumaki, David J. Lewis; Alex Terzich, Israel Kandarian, Alan Smart,
    Hye-Young Chung, Hilary Zaic, Maya Galbis, James Bennett, Michael Tyre
Support provided by: Autodesk Inc., Car-Freshner Corporation, Tavola S.P.A., and Wunder-Baum AG
Supporting architectural firms: Beyer Blinder Belle, Costas Kondylis & Partners, Fox & Fowle Architects,
    Gensler, Kaplan McLaughlin Diaz, Kohn Pedersen Fox Associates, Murphy/Jahn Architects, NBBJ,
    Pei Cobb Freed & Partners, Cesar Pelli & Associates, Perkins Eastman Architects
Photographer: Elliott Kaufman

Park Tower Speculative Project, 2004
Commissioned by: *Architectural Record* for the U.S. Pavilion, Venice Biennale
Project team: Paul Lewis, Marc Tsurumaki, David J. Lewis; Alex Terzich, Israel Kandarian, Michael Tyre,
    Hye-Young Chung, Hilary Zaic, Maya Galbis

Fluff Bakery, 2003–4, New York, NY -
Client: Chow Down Management Inc.
Project team: Paul Lewis, Marc Tsurumaki, David J. Lewis; Eric Samuels, project architect; James Bennett,
    Lucas Cascardo, Alex Terzich, Alan Smart, Maya Galbis, Hilary Zaic, Michael Tyre, Matthew Roman, Ana Ivascu
Contractor: Real Time Inc.
Photographer: Michael Moran

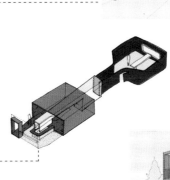

Bellow, 2004, in the Voting Booth Project, Parsons School of Design, New York, NY
Client: Parsons The New School of Design
Curator: Chee Pearlman
Exhibit conceived by: André Balazs, Rick Finkelstein, Paul Goldberger, Ken Lerer
Project team: Paul Lewis, Marc Tsurumaki, David J. Lewis; Alex Terzich, project architect; Matthew Roman
Photographer: Michael Moran

Xing Restaurant, 2003–5, New York, NY -
Client: Michael Lagudis and Chow Down Management Inc.
Project team: Paul Lewis, Marc Tsurumaki, David J. Lewis; Eric Samuels, project architect; Lucas Cascardo,
    Alex Terzich, Matthew Roman, Katherine Hearey, Adam Frampton
Mechanical engineer: Jack Green Associates
Contractor: Gateway Design Group
Photographer: Michael Moran

Gym Garage, 2005, Southampton, NY -
Client: Constantine Alexakos
Project team: Paul Lewis, Marc Tsurumaki, David J. Lewis; Lucas Cascardo, Robert Troy Schaum

Wieden + Kennedy Offices Renovation, 2005, New York, NY -
Client: Wieden + Kennedy
Project team: Paul Lewis, Marc Tsurumaki, David J. Lewis; Lucas Cascardo, project architect; Matthew Roman,
    Alex Terzich, Hilary Zaic, Beatie Blakemore, Erik Gerlach
Millwork: Nordic Interiors
Mechanical engineer: Laszlo Bodak Engineer

Tides Restaurant, 2004–5, New York, NY -
Client: Steven Yee and Allen Leung
Project team: Paul Lewis, Marc Tsurumaki, David J. Lewis; Lucas Casardo, project architect;
    Matthew Roman, Beatie Blakemore, Jeanie Lee
Contractor: Mao Nan Construction
Photographer: Michael Moran

Prototype Dormitory Room, 2005
Commissioned by: *Newsweek*
Project team: Paul Lewis, Marc Tsurumaki, David J. Lewis; Michael Tyre, Hilary Zaic, Maya Galbis,
    Matthew Roman

Dash Dogs Restaurant, 2005, New York, NY
Client: Steven Yee, Allen Leung, Dan Sook
Project team: Paul Lewis, Marc Tsurumaki, David J. Lewis; Alan Smart, Katherine Hearey, Adam Frampton,
    John Morrison, Chris Dierks, Tal Schori, David Snyder, Santiago Rivera Robles-Martinez,
    Monica Suberville, John Bassett, Erik Gerlach
Photographer: Michael Moran

Harley-Davidson Traveling Exhibitions, 2005–6 - - - - - - - - - - - - - - - - - -
Client: Harley-Davidson USA
Project manager: Ileen Sheppard Gallagher
Project team: Paul Lewis, Marc Tsurumaki, David J. Lewis; Alex Terzich, Hilary Zaic
Graphic design: Pure+Applied
Fabrication: Veyko

Bio-Medical Center Renovation, 2005–6, Brown University, Providence, RI -
Client: Brown University
Project team: Paul Lewis, Marc Tsurumaki, David J. Lewis; Lucas Cascardo, project architect;
    Robert Troy Schaum, Matthew Roman, Hilary Zaic
Construction manager: Shawmut Design and Construction
Graphic design: Pure+Applied

Parking Sections Re-installation, 2006, in Transcending Type, Yale School of Architecture Gallery, - - - - - - - -
    New Haven, CT
Curators: *Architectural Record*
Exhibition director: Dean Sakamoto
Project team: Paul Lewis, Marc Tsurumaki, David J. Lewis; Breanna Carlson, project manager; Chris Dierks,
    Santiago Rivera Robles-Martinez
Support provided by: Autodesk, Inc.

Parallel Lines Wallcovering Collection for Knoll Textiles, 2005–6, released June 2006
Client: Knoll Textiles
Project team: Paul Lewis, Marc Tsurumaki, David J. Lewis; Alex Terzich, project manager; Vivian Lee

The Green House Exhibition, 2005–6, National Building Museum, Washington DC -
Client: National Building Museum
Curators: Donald Albrecht, Christopher Hawthorne, Alanna Stang
Project team: Paul Lewis, Marc Tsurumaki, David J. Lewis; John Morrison, project manager;
    Alex Terzich, Matthew Roman, Monica Suberville
Graphic Design: Pure+Applied
Fabrication: National Building Museum
Photographer: Gretchen Franti-Hoachlander Davis Photography

Urban Outfitters Store, 2005–6, Durham, NC -
Client: Urban Outfitters
Project team: Paul Lewis, Marc Tsurumaki, David J. Lewis; Breanna Carlson, project architect; Hilary Zaic,
    Mia Lorenzetti, Matthew Roman, Monica Suberville
Architect of record: Ignarri-Lummis Architects
Contractor: Burda, Dunham, & Associates Corporation
Photographer: Ray Strawbridge

Urban Outfitters Store, 2005–6, Lynnwood, WA -
Client: Urban Outfitters
Project team: Paul Lewis, Marc Tsurumaki, David J. Lewis; Breanna Carlson, project architect;
    Hilary Zaic, Mia Lorenzetti, Monica Suberville
Architect of Record: D.A. Levy and Associates
Contractor: Robinson Construction

HPD Housing Development, 2004–6, East New York, NY -
Client: New York City Department of Housing, Preservation, and Development
Developer and Lead Architect: Just Green Development, LLC and Della Valle + Bernheimer Design
Collaborating firms: Architecture Research Office, BriggsKnowles Architecture + Design
Project team: Paul Lewis, Marc Tsurumaki, David J. Lewis; Eric Samuels, James Bennett, Lucas Cascardo
Structural engineer: Robert Silman Associates
Contractor: Triple Crown Construction

Building 82%, 2005–6, Miami Beach, FL -
Client: UIA Management LLC
Project team: Paul Lewis, Marc Tsurumaki, David J. Lewis; Marc Kushner, project architect;
    Monica Suberville, Hilary Zaic, Mia Lorenzetti, Tamicka Marcy
Landscape Architect: Raymond Jungles

Vegas 888 Spa and Skin, 2005–6, Las Vegas, NV
Client: Del American, Inc.
Project team: Paul Lewis, Marc Tsurumaki, David J. Lewis; Vivian Lee, project architect for Spa and Hot
    Spot; Marc Kushner, project architect for Sales Center; Alex Terzich, project architect for Sport
    Pavilion; Clark Manning, Matthew Roman, Tamicka Marcy, Santiago Rivera Robles-Martinez,
    Beatie Blakemore, Mia Lorenzetti, Alice Chun, Adam Frampton
Advertising and design: dbox
Structural engineer: Cary Kopczynski & Company
Mechanical engineer: Glumac
Lighting design: Lighting Design Alliance
Landscaping: Lifescapes International
Pool consultant: STO Design Group
Construction management: Construction Management & Development

Alexakos Townhouse, 2005–6, New York, NY -
Client: Constantine Alexakos
Project team: Paul Lewis, Marc Tsurumaki, David J. Lewis; Lucas Cascardo, project architect;
    Mia Lorenzetti, Matthew Roman
Structural engineer: Robert Silman Associates
Mechanical engineer: D'Antonio Engineering
General contractor: Black Cat Construction
Stair fabrication: Veyko

Arthouse at the Jones Center, 2005–, Austin, TX -
Client: Arthouse at the Jones Center-Contemporary Art for Texas
Project team: Paul Lewis, Marc Tsurumaki, David J. Lewis; Michael Tyre, project architect;
    Matthew Roman, Jason Dannenbring, Monica Suberville, Hilary Zaic, Tamicka Marcy, Mia Lorenzetti
Structural engineer: MJ Structures
Mechanical engineer: Kent Consulting Engineers
Lighting designer: Lightfield Inc.

Nazareth House, 2005–, Nazareth, PA -
Client: Dr. Toshi and Daina Tsurumaki
Project team: Paul Lewis, Marc Tsurumaki, David J. Lewis; Michael Tyre, Lucas Cascardo, Monica Suberville,
    Tamicka Marcy, Matthew Roman

Memorial Sloan-Kettering Lobby Wall, 2005–, New York, NY
Client: Memorial Sloan-Kettering
Art advisor: Nancy Rosen
Building architect: Skidmore, Owings and Merrill
Project team: Paul Lewis, Marc Tsurumaki, David J. Lewis; Alex Terzich, project manager;
    Jason Dannenbring, Matthew Roman

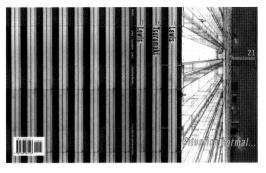

1993–1997

Awards
Best of Category, Environments, *I.D.* Magazine 41st Annual
Design Review, 1995. Slip Space
Selected Architect, Young Architects Forum, The Architectural
League of New York, 1997
Design Distinction, Environments, *I.D.* Magazine 43rd Annual
Design Review, 1997. Pull of Beauty
Honorable Mention, Environments, *I.D.* Magazine 43rd Annual
Design Review,1997. Eavesdropping

Projects
Container Building speculative project
Exquisite Corpse Clothing Store speculative project
Free Lobby/Block 1290 speculative project
Mies-on-a-beam speculative project
Skyfill Landfill speculative project
Sportbars speculative project
Video/Filmplex speculative project

Exhibitions
Slip Space, Storefront for Art and Architecture, NYC, 1994
Eavesdropping, Exit Art: The First World, NYC, 1996
Pull of Beauty, Storefront for Art and Architecture, NYC, 1996
Mantel Piece, Urban Center Galleries, NYC, 1997
Testing 1…2…3…, Storefront for Art and Architecture,
NYC, 1997

Publications
About LTL:
Butler, Connie. "Queer Space." *Art + Text* no. 49 (September
1994): 83–84. Slip Space
Codrington, Andrea. "'Pull of Beauty' at the Storefront for Art
and Architecture." *I.D. Magazine 43 Annual Design Review*,
July–August 1997, 149.
Codrington, Andrea. "'Eavesdropping' at Exit Art: The First
World." *I.D. Magazine 43 Annual Design Review*, July–
August 1997, 154.
Kotz, Liz. "Queer Spaces." *World Art*, November 1994, 114–15.
Slip Space
"Slipping Space at Storefront." *I.D. Magazine 41 Annual
Design Review*, July–August 1995, 148–50.

1998

Awards
The Mercedes T. Bass Rome Prize in Architecture, American
Academy in Rome, 1998–1999. Paul Lewis

Projects
Happy Mazza Media Company offices
Princeton Architectural Press offices
Van Alen Institute renovation

Exhibitions
Architecture @ the Edge of the Millennium, American
Academy in Rome, Italy, and NYC

Publications
By LTL:
Lewis.Tsurumaki.Lewis. *Situation Normal*… Pamphlet
Architecture 21. New York: Princeton Architectural
Press, 1998.

About LTL:
"Lewis.Tsurumaki.Lewis." *Oculus*, October 1998, 5.

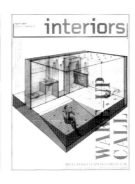

1999

Awards
Sportbars and Mies-on-a-Beam installed in the permanent collection, Architecture and Design, San Francisco Museum of Modern Art
Design Distinction, Environments, *I.D.* Magazine 45th Annual Design Review. Van Alen Institute

Projects
Carson Apartment
Everest Partners LLC Offices

Exhibitions
Snafu, Parsons School of Design Gallery, NYC
ReInstalled, AAM Architettura Arte Moderna, Rome, Italy
Three Rome Speculations, American Academy in Rome, Rome, Italy

Lectures
American Academy in Rome
Tyler School of Art

Publications
About LTL:
"Division of Labour." *Architectural Review,* July 1999, 86–87. Van Alen Institute
Donadio, Rachel. "Through American Eyes: A Wry Look at Rome." *International Herald Tribune,* 7 July 1999, 3.
Kellog, Craig. "Offices that Work: Modular Squad." *Working Woman,* February 1999, 58. Princeton Architectural Press
Schwartz, Bonnie. "The Van Alen Effect." *Interiors,* October 1999, 64–5.
"Van Alen Institute." *I.D. Magazine 45 Annual Design Review,* July–August 1999, 179.

2000

Awards
Selected Architects, "The New Vanguard," *Architectural Record*
Award and Grant, New York Foundation for the Arts
Faculty Design Award, The Association of Collegiate Schools of Architecture. Van Alen Institute
New Suburbanism installed in the permanent collection, Architecture and Design, The San Francisco Museum of Modern Art

Projects
Alexakos House
Geltner Loft
New Suburbanism speculative project

Exhibitions
Experiments: Recent Acquisitions of the Permanent Collection of Architecture and Design, San Francisco Museum of Modern Art, San Francisco, CA
Faculty Exhibit, Cornell University, Hartell Gallery, Cornell, NY
Refiled, National Design Triennial, The Cooper-Hewitt National Design Museum, New York, NY
10 Shades of Green, Urban Center Galleries, The Architectural League, New York, NY

Lectures
Catholic University of America
Drury University
New Jersey Institute of Technology
NYU Tisch School of Art

Publications
About LTL:
Albrecht, Donald, Ellen Lupton, and Steven Skov Holt. *Design Culture Now: National Design Triennial.* New York: Princeton Architectural Press, 2000: 134–35.
Cash, Stephanie. "Design: Sleeker, Thinner, Sexier." *Art in America,* July 2000, 50–53. Refiled
Giovannini, Joseph. "CityScape-Best Bytes." *New York,* 27 March 2000, 32–37. Refiled
Hales, Linda. "Forms that Put the Fun Back in Function." *Washington Post,* 11 March 2000, c1–c3. Refiled
Pearson, Clifford. "Design Culture Now." *Architectural Record,* April 2000, 74–80. Refiled
Stephens, Suzanne. "Design Vanguard: Lewis.Tsurumaki. Lewis explores ways of making the familiar strange." *Architectural Record,* December 2000, 116–99.

2001

Projects
The Architectural League of New York Offices
Essex Street Studios
Prototype Hotel Room
Upside House

Exhibitions
Snafu, University of Pennsylvania School of Architecture, Dean's Gallery, Philadelphia, PA
Architecture + Water, Van Alen Institute, NYC

Lectures
Nashville Cultural Arts Project
Ohio State University
State University of New York, Stony Brook
University of Oregon, Portland
University of Oregon, Eugene
University of Pennsylvania
Van Alen Institute

Publications
By LTL:
Lewis.Tsurumaki.Lewis. "New Suburbanism." *Ai: Architecture and Ideas,* Spring 2001, 72–79.

About LTL:
Bell, Jonathan. "Destination Unknown." In *Carchitecture,* 122–23. Basel: Birkhauser, 2001. New Suburbanism and Tourbus Hotel
Howeler, Eric. "Soft Serve: Etekt.com and House_N." *Praxis* 3 (2001): 96–103. Upside House
"Interview with Lewis.Tsurumaki.Lewis." *Van Alen Report* 9 (May 2001): 9–25.
Muschamp, Herbert. "Instant Inspiration: Just Add Water." *New York Times,* 6 April 2001, sect. E, p. 33–34. Architecture + Water
"No Reservations." *Interiors,* March 2001, cover, 100–01. Prototype Hotel Room
Pratt, Kevin. "The Coast is Clear." *Time Out New York,* 19 April 2001, 56. Architecture + Water
Rappaport, Nina. "An Architecture in the Making: Young Architects in New York." *tec21* 8 (23 February 2001): 7–18. Slip Space, Lozoo Restaurant, and Refiled
"Simples e Portatil." *Arquitetura & Urbanismo,* February–March 2001, 18. Princeton Architectural Press
Sirefman, Susanna. *New York: A Guide to Recent Architecture.* London: Ellipsis, 2001: 5.4–5.5. Van Alen Institute

2002

Awards

Kalil Memorial Fellowship, to support research on Invernizzi's Girasole, Verona

New Suburbanism installed in the permanent collection, The Heinz Architectural Center at the Carnegie Museum of Art

Selected Architects, Emerging Voices, The Architectural League of New York

Projects

Davies Penthouse

Great Egyptian Museum Competition

Lozoo Restaurant

Tourbus Hotel speculative project

Exhibitions

Architecture + Water
UCLA, Department of Architecture, Los Angeles, CA
San Francisco Museum of Modern Art, San Francisco, CA
The Heinz Architectural Center, Carnegie Museum of Art, Pittsburgh, PA

Negotiating Domesticity: Inquiry into Contemporary Suburban Residential Design, The Greenwich Arts Council, Greenwich, CA

Big Brother: Architecture and Surveillance, National Museum of Contemporary Art, Athens, Greece

Three Dimensions of Architecture, The Rachofsky House, Dallas, TX

2x2, The University of Texas at Austin School of Architecture, Austin, TX

Satirical Efficiencies, University of Virginia, Charlottesville, VA

New Hotels for Global Nomads, Cooper-Hewitt National Design Museum, New York, NY

Lectures

Emerging Voices, The Architectural League of New York

Carnegie Museum of Art

The Cooper Union for the Advancement of Science and Art

Rhode Island School of Design

Southern California Institute of Architecture

University of California, Berkeley

University of Nevada, Las Vegas

University of Texas, Austin

University of Toronto

University of Virginia

Publications

By LTL:

Lewis, David J. "Newness, Play, and Invention." *Scapes* 1 (2002): 20–21.

Lewis.Tsurumaki.Lewis. "Tourbus Hotel." In *Big Brother: Architecture and Surveillance*, 54–61. Athens: EMET, 2002.

About LTL:

Albrecht, Donald, and Elizabeth Johnson. "Lewis.Tsurumaki. Lewis. Tourbus Hotel." In *New Hotels for Global Nomads*, 76–9. New York: Merrel, 2002.

Filippis, Memos. "Big Brother, Architecture and Surveillance: Effective Affinities." In *Big Brother: Architecture and Surveillance*, 11–24. Athens: EMET, 2002. Tourbus Hotel

Hays, K. Michael, and Lauren Kogod, eds. "Twenty Projects at

the Boundaries of the Architectural Discipline Examined in Relation to the Historical and Contemporary Debates over Autonomy." *Perspecta* 33 (2002): 54–71. New Suburbanism

Litt, Steven. "Glorious Designs for Waterfronts Could Spark Ideas for Cleveland." *The Plain Dealer*, 17 March 2002, sect. J, p. 3. Architecture + Water

Lowry, Patricia. "Waterfront Fertile Plains for Design." *Pittsburgh Post-Gazette*, 14 February 2002. Architecture+ Water

Sardar, Zahid. "Beyond Convention: Three Shows Redefine the Boundaries of Architecture." *San Francisco Chronicle*, 21 December 2002. Architecture + Water

Tucker, Reed. "Zoo Station." *Time Out New York*, 17 October 2002, 52. Lozoo Restaurant

Turner, Rob. "Keeping the Lighting Turned Up and the Budget Down." *New York Times*, 17 October 2002, sect. D, p. 3. Lozoo Restaurant

2003

Awards

James Beard Foundation Award Nomination, Outstanding Restaurant Design. Lozoo Restaurant

Design Distinction, Environments, *I.D.* Magazine 49th Annual Design Review. Lozoo Restaurant

Projects

Perth Amboy High School Competition

Wooster House

World Trade Center Memorial Competition

Exhibitions

FAAR-Out: Six Months in Rome, The Art Directors Club, New York, NY

Light Structures, Syracuse University, Syracuse, NY

Lectures

Architectural Association of Ireland

California College of the Arts

Denver Architectural Lab

Kansas City AIA Young Architects Forum

Pennsylvania State University

Pratt Institute

San Francisco Museum of Modern Art

Syracuse University

University of North Carolina, Chapel Hill

Virginia Polytechnic Institute

Young Architect Forum, Copenhagen, Denmark

Publications

By LTL:

Lewis.Tsurumaki.Lewis. "New Suburbanism." *OZ* (Kansas State University) 25 (2003): 34–39.

Lewis.Tsurumaki.Lewis. "Perspecta 34: Temporary Architecture." Book Review. *Constructs* (Yale University), Fall 2003, 10.

Lewis.Tsurumaki.Lewis. "Suburbanism of Mass Customization." *Cornell Journal of Architecture* 7 (2003): 34–43.

Lewis.Tsurumaki.Lewis. "Tourbus Hotel." *Work in Progress* (Rhode Island School of Design) no. 8 (Fall 2003): 10–15.

Lewis.Tsurumaki.Lewis. "Upside House: Speculative House Design for Etekt.com." *Center: A Journal for Architecture in America* (University of Texas) no. 12 The Good Building (2003): 76–79.

About LTL:

Adam, Huburtus. "Van Alen Institute" and "Lozoo." In *New York Architecture and Design*, 52–53 and 120–21. New York: teNeues, 2003.

Beamon, Kelly. "Tour-Rific Hotel: A Museum Show Concept offers a Real-Life Solution." *Hospitality Design*, January–February 2003, 44–47. Tourbus Hotel

Brown, Bay. "Lewis.Tsurumaki.Lewis: Grand Egyptian Museum Competition." *Architecture*, May 2003, 62–63.

Kristal, Marc. "Linear Solution." *Metropolis*, October 2003, 44. Lozoo Restaurant

"Lozoo Chinese Kitchen." *I.D. Magazine 49 Annual*

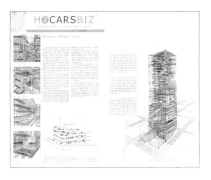

Design Review, July–August 2003, 119.

Luna, Ian. "Lozoo" and "Van Alen Institute." In *New New York: Architecture and a City*, 74–77 and 120–23. New York: Rizzoli, 2003.

Smiley, David J. "A Vertical Mixed-Use Suburb." In *Sprawl and Public Space, Redressing the Mall*, 74–75. Washington DC: NEA, 2002. New Suburbanism

Yang, Andrew. "04-Off the Shoulder." *Frame*, March–April 2003, 24. Lozoo Restaurant

2004

Awards

Selected Architects, Venice Biennale—U.S. Pavilion, September 2004

Interiors Award Winner, Restaurant, *Contract* magazine. Ini Ani Coffee Shop

Projects

Bornhuetter Hall
Fluff Bakery
Ini Ani Coffee Shop
Park Tower speculative project
Rotare Light
Seward Park Lobby competition

Exhibitions

Light Structures, University of Michigan, Ann Arbor, MI

Parking Sections, U.S. Pavilion, Venice Biennale, 9th International Architecture Exhibition

Bellow, in the Voting Booth Project, Parsons School of Design, New York, NY

Lectures

Colorado College
Columbia University
Princeton University
University of Michigan

Publications

About LTL:

"Bar en Carton." *Le Moniteur Architecture*, October 2004, 38. Ini Ani Coffee Shop

Beamon, Kelly. "Material World." *Hospitality Design*, July 2004, 17. Ini Ani Coffee Shop

Blair, Gwenda. "Designers Redefine the Political Machine." *New York Times*, 7 October 2004, sect. F, p. 7. Bellow

Boyer, Jennifer. "All Things Familiar: Architectural Process as a Means for Invention." *Building Material: The Architectural Association of Ireland*, Spring 2004, 53–54. New Suburbanism and Video/Filmplex

Cuito, Aurora. "Lozoo Restaurant," and "Geltner/Parker Loft." In *New York Minimalism*, 48–53, 118–25. New York: Harper Design International, 2004.

Fischer, Joachim, ed. "Lozoo Restaurant." In *Restaurant Design*, 254–63. Köln: daab gmbh, 2004.

Galadza, Sofia. "Material: In the Mix." *Contract*, December 2004, 30–31. Tides Restaurant and Xing Restaurant

"Geltner/Parker Loft." In *New Kitchen Design*, 112–15. Köln: Daab gmbh, 2004.

Guiney, Anne. "From Deep Space to Office Space." *Architect's Newspaper*, 21 September 2004, 3. Rotare

Herbers, Jill. "UpSide House." In *Prefab Modern*, 138–39. New York: Harper Design, 2004.

Ho, Cathy Lang. "The Metamorph of Venice." *Architect's Newspaper*, 13 July 2004, 1–5. Parking Sections.

Holtzman, Anna. "Interior Design, No Appointment Necessary." *New York Times*, 15 April 2004, sect., F, p. 4. Ini Ani Coffee Shop

"Hydrogen Park Tower." *H2CarsBiz* 2, no. 4 (2004): 16–17. Park Tower

Ivy, Robert. "On the Road to Venice: 9th Architecture

Biennale." *Architectural Record*, November 2004, 91–119. Parking Sections

Kasuga, Yoshiko. "Ini Ani Coffee Shop." *SPA-DE: Space and Design* 2 (2004): 106–8.

Kristal, Marc. "Divide and Conquer." *Metropolis*, May 2004, 74–78. Essex Street Studios

"Lewis.Tsurumaki.Lewis/Ini Ani." *Monitor* no. 27 (2004): 61.

"Light Construction." *Surface* no. 51 (2004): 85. Rotare

"Lozoo Restaurant." *Lighting Today* 1 (2004): cover and 50–53.

Lubell, Sam. "Architectural Record Curating Venice Architecture Biennale's American Pavilion." *Architectural Record*, August 2004, 32. Parking Sections

Minutillo, Josephine. "Manhattan's Cardboard Café." *Azure*, September–October 2004, 58.

Minutillo, Josephine. "Share and Share I Like: Essex Street Studio." *Architectural Record*, January 2004, 50.

Pearson, Clifford A. "For the pint-size Ini Ani Coffee Shop in Lower Manhattan, Lewis.Tsurumaki.Lewis reinvents the java-sipping experience." *Architectural Record*, September 2004, 118–21.

Quinton, Maryse. "Europe Hotels." *Le Moniteur Architecture*, December 2004, 125.

Riding, Alan. "Exploring Design as Metamorphosis." *New York Times*, 15 September 2004, sect. E, p. 1.

Serrats, Marta. "Geltner/Parker Loft." In *Big Designs for Small Kitchens*, 36–39. New York: Harper Design International, 2004.

Way, James. "Tiny Café, Huge Design." *Architect's Newspaper*, 11 May 2004, 5.

Yang, Andrew. "The New New Yorkers." **Surface* no. 50 (October 2004): 150.

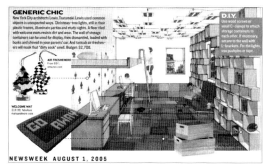

2005

Awards

Winner, Casual Restaurant, First Annual Hospitality Design Awards for Creative Achievement, *Hospitality Design* magazine. Fluff Bakery

Design Distinction, Environments, *I.D.* Magazine 51st Annual Design Review. Ini Ani Coffee Shop

Winner, Interiors Awards, Restaurant, *Contract* magazine. Tides Restaurant

Selected Winner, New York Designs, The Architectural League of New York

Design Merit Award, Interior Architecture, AIA New York Chapter. Xing Restaurant

Design Merit Award, Projects, AIA New York Chapter. Park Tower

Finalist, Casual Dining, *Interior Design* Gold Key Awards. Tides Restaurant and Fluff Bakery

Honorable Mention, The AR Awards for Emerging Architecture, *Architectural Review*. Tides Restaurant

Projects

Dash Dogs Restaurant
Gym Garage
Prototype Dormitory Room
Tides Restaurant
Wieden + Kennedy Offices renovation
Xing Restaurant

Exhibitions

Restricted Play, Parsons School of Design, New York, NY
Light Structures, Northeastern University, Boston, MA
Park Tower and New Suburbanism in Cities—10 Lines: Approaches to City and Open Territory Design, Harvard University Graduate School of Design, Cambridge, MA

Lectures

ACSA Keynote Lecture, Detroit, Michigan
Architecture Talks, Lucerne, Switzerland
Baltimore AIA
Dallas Architecture Forum
DDI Color Material Specifiers Conference
Florida Atlantic University
Georgia Institute of Technology
Lawrence Technological University
Miami University, Ohio
New York Designs, The Architectural League of New York
Northeastern University
Parsons School of Design
University at Buffalo, The State University of New York
University of Colorado
University of Tennessee
University of Texas, Austin
Wesleyan University

Publications

By LTL:

Lewis.Tsurumaki.Lewis. "Invernizzi's Exquisite Corpse: The Villa Girasole: An Architecture of Surrationalism." In *Surrealism and Architecture*, edited by Thomas Mical, 156–67. New York: Routledge, 2005.

Tsurumaki, Marc. "From the Known to the Unknown." *Volume* 1 (2005).

About LTL:

"03: Food > Fluff Bakery // New York." *Monitor* no. 30 (2005): 34–37.

"Architectural Design: restaurant > Tides // New York." *Monitor* no. 32 (2005): 62–65.

"Art to Go." *Better Homes and Gardens*, September 2005, 144. Ini Ani Coffee Shop

Barton, David. "Create a Gym: Second Place: Sport Bars." *New York Magazine*, 7 February 2005, 14–15. Sportsbars.

Braham, Bill. "Zoom In: Ivalo Lighting: Ivalo > Rotare." *Monitor* no. 33 (2005): 100–01.

Faires, Robert. "Movin' On Up." *Austin Chronicle*, 29 July 2005. Arthouse at the Jones Center

"FILE Filing New Openings Worldwide: Smart Spaces that House Quality Product: Fluff Bakery." *Monitor* no. 33 (2005): 136–37.

"First Annual Hospitality Design Awards: Winner Casual Restaurant, Fluff." *Hospitality Design*, July 2005, 82–83.

"Fluff: Open Bakery." *Architect's Newspaper*, 2 February 2005, 3.

Galadza, Sofia. "The 26th Annual Interiors Awards: Restaurant: Ini Ani Coffee Shop." *Contract*, January 2005, 90–91.

"Generic Chic." *Newsweek*, 1 August 2005, 57–58. Prototype Dormitory Room

Gilstrap, Michelle. "Coffee with Sugar and Comfort." *DDI Magazine*, February 2005, 22. Ini Ani Coffee Shop

Gregory, Rob. "Shifting Tides." *Architectural Review*, December 2005, 85.

Gross, Jamie. "Winning Streaks." *Surface* no. 53 (2005): 60. Fluff Bakery

Hagberg, Eva. "Currents: To Protect Their Projects, Young Architects Try DIY." *New York Times*, 10 March 2005, sect. F, p. 3. Tides Restaurant and Xing Restaurant

Hagberg, Eva. "Seeing Stars and Sea Anemones: Around the Corner, Xing and Tides by Lewis.Tsurumaki.Lewis." *Oculus* 67, no. 2 (Spring 2005): 21.

Hall, Peter. "Rotare: Lewis.Tsurumaki.Lewis." *Metropolis*, June 2005, 180–81.

Kagelmann, Boris. "From Inside to Out." *Jam* (Autumn/Winter 2005): 4–9. Various projects

Kasuga, Yoshiko. "Fluff Bakery." *SPA-DE: Space and Design* 3 (2005): 45–47. Ini Ani Coffee Shop and Fluff Bakery.

Kasuga, Yoshiko. "New York Restaurant Designers." *Viewer* 1 (2005): 108–13.

Kasuga, Yoshiko. "Tides," and "Xing." *SPA-DE: Space and Design* 4 (2005): 70–72.

Krisanakreingkrai, Vimorat. "Strip Tease." *Art4D* (October 2005): 70–72. Fluff Bakery

"Lewis.Tsurumaki.Lewis: Architectural Opportunism." *Dimensions* (University of Michigan) 18 (2005): 88–95. Various projects

"Lewis.Tsurumaki.Lewis: Xing Restaurant, Fluff Bakery, Ini Ani Coffee Shop, Bornhuetter Hall." *MARU Interior Design*, April 2004, cover and 50–65.

Mastrelli, Tara. "Horizontal Vertigo." *Hospitality Design*, April 2005, 164–67. Fluff Bakery

McKee, Bradford. "The New College Mixer." *New York Times*, 1 September 2005, sect. F, p. 1. Bornhuetter Hall

McKeough, Tim. "In Three Manhattan Restaurants." *Icon* no. 25 (July 2005): 39–40. Fluff Bakery, Tides Restaurant, and Xing Restaurant

"The Midas Touch." *Interior Design*, October 2005, 186. Tides Restaurant and Xing Restaurant

Montrucchio, Noel. "A Bite of the Big Apple." *Spaces* no. 13 (2005): 100–03. Various projects

Moreno, Shonquis. "The Space: The Literal Zone." *Frame* no. 46 (September–October 2005): 154–57. Tides Restaurant

Pogrebin, Robin. "New York's New Architecture District." *New York Times*, 21 August 2005, sect. 2, pp. 26–27. Essex Street Studios

Rieselbach, Anne. "What's the Big Plan?" *Oculus* 67, no. 4 (Fall 2005): 36–37. Tides Restaurant

Rodger, Nelda, and Elizabeth Pagliacolo. "Global Trends: Inspired by Nature." *Azure*, October 2005, 78. Tides Restaurant

Roy, Sree. "Material Guys." *Display Design Ideas*, July 2005, 36–38. Fluff Bakery and Tides Restaurant

Ryan, Zoë. "Detail 01: Bread and Butter." *Frame* no. 44 (May–June 2005): 21–22. Fluff Bakery

Seward, Aaron. "Dining Duo, New York City." *Architectural Lighting*, May–June 2005, 48–49.

Singh, Karen D. "Labworks, Materials Study: Lewis.Tsurumaki.Lewis." *Interior Design*, March 2005, 121–22.

"Wave of the Future." *Hospitality Design*, October 2005, 114–27. Various projects

Wines, Suzan. "Dionysius in New York." *Domus Speciale*, April 2005, 34–39. Various projects

Yang, Andrew. "Triple Ingenuity." *Metropolis*, May 2005, cover and 140–44. Various projects

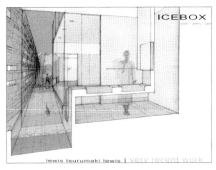

2006

Awards

Design Award, Project Citation, AIA New York Chapter. Nazareth House

Honorable Mention, Casual Restaurant, Second Annual Hospitality Design Awards for Creative Achievements, *Hospitality Design* magazine. Dash Dogs

Projects

Alexakos Townhouse
Arthouse at the Jones Center (ongoing)
Bio-Medical Center renovation
Building 82%
HPD Housing Development
Memorial Sloan-Kettering Lobby Wall (ongoing)
Nazareth House (ongoing)
Parallel Lines Wallcovering Collection for Knoll Textiles
Urban Outfitters stores
Vegas 888 Skin and Spa

Exhibitions

Light Structures, Kent State University, Kent, OH
Very Recent Work, Icebox Gallery, Syracuse, NY
Harley Davidson Traveling Exhibitions
The Green House Exhibition, National Building Museum, Washington DC
Parking Sections in Transcending Type, Yale School of Architecture Gallery, New Haven, CT

Lectures

AIA Florida Emerging Professionals Conference
Autonomous University of Nuevo Leon, Monerrey, Mexico
California Polytechnic State University, San Luis Obispo
Catholic University
Kent State University
Louisiana Tech University
North Carolina State University
Rice University
University of British Columbia
University of Nebraska
Virginia Commonwealth University
Yale University

Publications

About LTL:

Bergmans, Jeroen. "Room for Change." *Wallpaper*, October 2006, 122. Park Tower

Bernstein, Fred A. "Architecture New Designs." *Princeton Alumni Weekly*, 25 January 2006, 47. Various projects

"The Big Picture: Fluff Bakery, New York." *Commercial Interior Design* (Dubai), May 2006, 64.

Bisbal, Cristina. "Tides Restaurant." *Diseñ Art Magazine* no. 6 (2006): 164.

Chen, Aric. "Experimental Architects Draft New Looks for the Wall." *New York Times*, 29 June 2006, F3. Parallel Lines

Dann, Ying-Lan. "Space Craft." *Monument*, April–May 2006, 10, 14, 88. Fluff Bakery and Dash Dogs

Dodge, Stephen. "Ordinary Tactics." *Architecture BC* (Summer 2006), 32–33. Various projects

"Effect > fast food > dash dogs // new york." *Monitor* no. 37 (2006): 94–97.

"Finalist Casual or Quickservice Restaurant: Dash Dogs." *Hospitality Design*, July 2006, 86, 125.

Galadza, Sofia. "Small Restaurant: Tides." *Contract*, January 2006, 96–97.

Gardiner, Virginia. "Design, Build, and Beyond." *Dwell*, February–March 2006, 152–64.

Hand, Gunnar. "The New Urbanism." *Architect's Newspaper*, 21 June 2006, 8. Urban Outfitters

"Interiors: International." *Interiors Korea*, October 2006, 198–215. Various projects

"Interiors MERIT: Xing Restaurant," and " Projects MERIT: Park Tower," *Oculus Special Issue*, 2006, 32, 40.

Jodido, Philip. "Dash Dogs." In *Minimum Space Maximum Living*. Victoria: Images Publishing Group, 2006. 50–53.

Jodidio, Philip. "Fluff Bakery," and "Bornhuetter Hall." In *Architecture Now 4*, 274–381. London: Taschen, 2006.

Kasuga, Yoshiko. "Dash Dogs." *SPA-DE: Space and Design* 5 (2006): 116–17.

Lim, Cj. "Bellow.Lewis.Tsurumaki.Lewis" and "Eavesdropping. Lewis.Tsurumaki.Lewis." *Devices: A Manual of Architectural and Spatial Machines*. Oxford: Architectural Press, 2006: 28–29, 64–65.

Marull, Kina. "Panaderia Fluff." *Diseñ Art Magazine* no. 7 (2006): cover, 158–59.

Moreno, Shonquis. "Dash In, Dash Out." *Frame* no. 50 (May/June 2006) 40.

Moreno, Shonquis. "Follow the Ribbon." *Mark* no. 4 (Fall 2006): 53. Xing Restaurant

Oppenheimer Dean, Andrea. "Living the Green Life: A Quest for Affordable and Beautiful Sustainability." *Architectural Record*, August 2006, 45–46. Green House exhibition

"Parallel Line Collection: Knoll Textiles." *L.A. Architect*, October 2006, 14.

"Project Citation: Nazareth House." *Oculus* 68, no. 4 (Fall 2006): 31.

Rappaport, Nina. "Marc Tsurumaki." *Constructs Architecture*, Fall 2006, 5.

Riordan, John. "Tides" and "Xing." In *Restaurants by Design*, 16–23, 92–99. New York: Collins Design and Grayson Publications, 2006.

Schiowitz, Jana. "A few of their favorite things." *Hospitality Design*, March 2006, 65. Dash Dogs

"Scope: Fluff Bakery, Tides Restaurant, Xing Restaurant, *IW Magazine* (Taiwan), Summer 2006, 52–64.

Singer, Jill. "New + Notable for 2006." *I.D.*, December 2006, 108. Parallel Lines

Singh, Karen D. "Lighting: Ivalo Lighting." *Interior Design*, April 2006, 130. Rotare

Snyder, Tim. "Green Building Goes on Tour." *Fine Homebuilding*, September 2006, 16–18. Green House exhibition

"Tides." *Interior + Design Magazine* (Russia), Summer 2006, 46.

Von Arx, Irina. "Il cuoco, l'artigiano e l'architetto." *Domus*, April 2006, 42–47. Dash Dogs and Xing Restaurant

Weathersby, Jr., William. "Lewis.Tsurumaki.Lewis Turns the Tables on an Oddly Shaped Space Fashioning Xing in New York City." *Architectural Record*, March 2006, 187, 198–201.

"The Writing's on the Wallpaper." *Architectural Record*, August 2006, 191. Parallel Lines

"Xing Restaurant." *Europaconcorsi Portfolio* (April 2006): www.europaconcorsi.com.

Staff

Michael Tyre

Alex Terzich

Julian Rose

Jason Dannenbring

Steven Hong

Carolynn Karp

Adam Frampton

David J. Lewis

Marc Tsurumaki

Paul Lewis

Maya Galbis

Troy Schaum

Alan Smart

Vivian Lee

Mia Lorenzetti

Santiago Rivera Robles-Martinez

Breanna Carlson

Deane Simpson

Matt Roman

Clement Valla

Marc Kushner

Elizabeth Hodges

Tamicka Marcy

Clark Manning

Hilary Zaic

Stephanie Tuerk

Brian Ha

Katherine Hearey

Diana Martinez

Jason Tang

Sima Rustom

James Bennett

David Takacs

Lucas Cascardo

Monica Suberville

Eric Samuels

Hye-Young Chung

Israel Kandarian

Acknowledgments

We are grateful for the extraordinarily talented and creative people who have been collaborators in the office of Lewis.Tsurumaki.Lewis. They have each contributed enormously to the work represented in this book, engaging each project with professionalism, intelligence, and wit, even acting as human entourage when necessary in the pursuit of opportunistic architecture.

We thank our colleagues and students, past and present, at the institutions through which we have had the opportunity to engage in lively dialogue and spirited exchange over the critical value of architecture, culture, and history at Princeton University, Columbia University, Parsons The New School for Design, Cornell University, Yale University, University of Pennsylvania, Ohio State University, Barnard College, and NJIT. We particularly acknowledge the heads of these institutions' architecture programs for their support: Stan Allen, Michael Cadwell, Mark Cruvellier, Karen Fairbanks, Urs Gauchat, Kent Hubbell, Kent Kleinman, Ralph Lerner, Joeb Moore, Robert A. M. Stern, Karen Van Lengen, Anthony Vidler, Richard Wesley, Peter Wheelwright, and Mark Wigley. LTL followed an earlier collaboration with Peter Pelsinski, to whom we express our continuing admiration and friendship. We thank our many colleagues in the Essex Street Studios with whom we have shared space, time, and ideas, including Eric Bunge and Mimi Hoang, Laura Briggs and Jonathan Knowles, Beth Weinstein, Gundula Proksch, Srdjan Jovanovic Weiss, Makram el Kadi, Ziad Jamaleddine and Naji Moujaes.

We extend our appreciation and respect for the individuals in whose offices we had the privilege of working prior to establishing LTL, notably Elizabeth Diller, Ricardo Scofidio, Joel Sanders, and Peter Guggenheimer. Kyong Park and Shirin Neshat at Storefront for Art and Architecture; Rosalie Genevro and Anne Reiselbach at the Architectural League of New York; Ray Gastil at Van Alen Institute; Suzanne Stephens, Clifford Pearson, and Robert Ivy at *Architectural Record*; Tracy Myers at the Heinz Architectural Center; and Donald Albrecht have graciously given us opportunity and provocation for public presentations of our work.

Special thanks to Kevin Lippert and Clare Jacobson of Princeton Architectural Press for their support over the years. Dorothy Ball provided critical advice in the development of the text of this book, and Jan Haux extended a discerning eye on its composition. We are thankful to have had the privilege of collaborating with Michael Moran on the photography of our work, and we benefit from his exceptional awareness of the interplay between architecture and image.

And finally, we are indebted to the lifelong encouragement, patience, and even prodding of our families—Beth Irwin Lewis, Arnold Lewis, Martha Lewis, Toshi Tsurumaki, Daina Tsurumaki, and Chris Tsurumaki.

This book is dedicated to:
Kim Yao and Sarabeth Lewis Yao
    —Paul Lewis
Carmen Lenzi, Kai Luca Tsurumaki, and Lucia Alise Tsurumaki
    —Marc Tsurumaki
Alice Min Soo Chun and Quinn Arnold Lewis
    —David J. Lewis

Lewis.Tsurumaki.Lewis (LTL)

is an architecture partnership established in New York City in 1997 by Marc Tsurumaki and twin brothers Paul Lewis and David J. Lewis.

Paul Lewis is Assistant Professor at Princeton University. Marc Tsurumaki is Adjunct Professor at Columbia University. David J. Lewis is Associate Professor at Parsons The New School for Design.